Contents

Bibliography

Heap B, *Degree Course Offers 2009 Entry*, London, Trotman
Widmer, J, *The Penguin Careers Guide 2006* (13th edition), London, Penguin

Introduction

Since first writing this book in 2008, many things have changed. Some of these changes – like the number of universities you can apply to being reduced from six to five – were included in the 2010 edition, but inevitably there have been more changes with a new government and an increase in the fees students will pay from 2012. There has been massive publicity about this and many sixth-formers may now be reconsidering taking a university course. However, please don't be put off applying to university if you come from a low-income household. There are grants and bursaries to help you, as outlined in the last chapter.

Nevertheless, you will now need to consider if you want to accumulate so much debt and whether a degree is the best route for the career you have in mind – that is if you have an idea of what you would like to do!

This guide is for any pupil – and their parents and advisers – thinking of applying to university. From as early as Year 11 (and even before for those who really plan in advance!) there are practical things you can be doing to make sure your application goes more smoothly and to ensure that you have done everything you can to show yourself in the best light possible.

Apart from your academic studies, which are obviously very important, you need to show the people who are making decisions about your future how much you have to offer in other areas. For instance, you may be heading for a science degree but you play the guitar and have several music grades to your name.

Whatever you have done in an extracurricular way helps to show what you are like as a person, and not just as an exam candidate. So before you think about what you would like to do in the future, think about what you have achieved in the past. Be positive about yourself. Think about your strengths and acknowledge weaknesses in a positive way. This will help you later when you have to prepare your personal statement on the UCAS form.

Applying to university can seem daunting with over 300 institutions offering more than 50,000 courses. You, however, will have to bring your choice down to only five places! Don't worry though – when you make your application on the UCAS form, your choices will be listed alphabetically so each institution won't know where else you have applied to or what your first choice may be.

Each chapter in this guide takes you through the process of your UCAS application, from thinking about the subjects which interest you and the courses which might appeal, to choosing your five universities and, most importantly, the writing of your personal statement. The advantages – and disadvantages – of taking a gap year are explained and there is guidance on what to expect in interviews and how to make the most of them. There is advice and information on what to do when your results arrive and some tips on dealing with finance.

Throughout the book I have included the experiences of young people who are currently at or applying for university, and the personal statements are just as they appeared on the UCAS application.

Everything is done online and although you will be able to access the UCAS site at school and make your application, it may be that the time on computers is limited. If your family does not have a personal computer with Internet access, you can make use of the facilities at your local library or career centre. If there is any problem with lack of access please discuss this with your form teacher who should be able to make sure you have enough time at a computer in school.

Parents and advisers reading this book should get a far greater insight into the university system. You may not have been to university, but even if you have the application processes have changed! In this guide you will find all the advice and information you need to help your child (or pupils) make their choices with confidence. You may have to nag to get them to complete tasks on time, but it will be worth it in the long run.

Disclaimer

All the dates mentioned in this book are correct at the time of going to press. Please refer to UCAS for confirmation, www.ucas.com.

Chapter One

Looking and Planning Ahead

Case study

'It would have been really useful to have had a timetable for parents. As soon as they entered Year 12 we seemed to miss things (for instance university visits) as it all seemed so distant at the time. It crept up on us rather alarmingly. Whilst the school was very good at assisting them, if the boys didn't tell us about what was going on, we didn't necessarily know what was happening, so we didn't keep them on track. I know it seems obvious now to have looked at the UCAS website, but at the time I wasn't aware I could do this and didn't think of using it to guide us through. I'm hoping that we'll be more organised the third time around!'

Fiona, mother of two sons at university, and one in the sixth form.

The first important dates

You will find a more comprehensive list of dates at the end of this book in Appendix 1, but here are the first dates that you should highlight. These dates are the same every year and are specific to students in Year 13 – the year of application.

- **September 2012** – You can start your application process.
- **15th October 2012** – Deadline for applications to University of Oxford, University of Cambridge and courses in medicine, dentistry and veterinary science or veterinary medicine.
- **15th January 2013** – Applications must be in to guarantee equal academic consideration.

Future careers

When you're thinking about applying to university, it helps if you have some idea of the sort of career you would like after you have graduated. However, that's the best-case scenario and very few pupils in Years 11, 12 and 13 actually have a firm idea about what areas they would eventually like to work in. Some do, of course, and some say they do, but frequently change their minds! Many students go to university to study a subject or combination of subjects that appeals to them, without any idea of future career prospects.

Sometimes when you are thinking about your future, it's just a question of knowing what you don't want to do that helps you focus on suitable careers. Some schools and colleges run computer-based psychometric tests to produce a list of careers and areas that might appeal to you. These may be helpful in the broader sense and some students have been quite surprised by the results!

You can also do the Stamford Test on the UCAS site. This short questionnaire is quick and easy to complete, and can help you think about your interests and abilities in relation to subjects you might like to study at university. You can complete this questionnaire before you register with UCAS – you only need to fill in a few personal details like name, date of birth and email address before you start the test.

'Many students go to university to study a subject or combination of subjects that appeals to them, without any idea of future career prospects.'

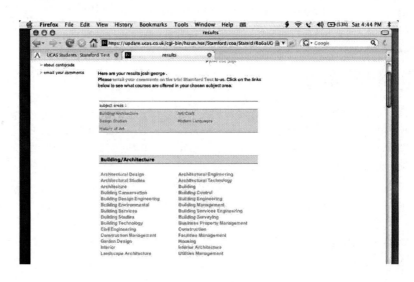

Josh, who is in Year 12 and is studying French, art, economics and politics, completed the Stamford Test (see opposite) and was interested to see that the results indicated architecture – a subject he had already thought about.

Which careers interest you?

Think about the jobs that appeal to you and start making notes in a file, on cards or on your computer. You can then check what qualifications are needed for these areas. Some careers just want a first degree in any subject but others are far more specific, so it's important to check.

For example, although there are now first degrees in journalism and media studies, entry into the profession can be by graduates of any discipline. To be a lawyer you don't have to study law but you will have to take a further qualification before proceeding to the Legal Practice Course (LPC) and articles.

Asking family and friends

You may start off being interested in a certain job because someone in your family or a person you know and admire is involved in that work. This is a good point of departure – talk to that person and ask them about their specific job, how long it took them to train, what qualifications they needed and so on. Even though entry qualifications may have changed, it will give you an idea of what's involved.

Next, you should ask them about related jobs in their sphere as these might also appeal to you and could be areas you've not considered before. For example, you may be interested in nursing but have not thought about physiotherapy or occupational health.

Ask your friends about what their parents do – if you don't know already – and ask to speak to them about their jobs. Don't be shy about this – most people are flattered by any interest in what they do, and they may be able to introduce you to other people who can provide more information.

Help from school or college

Make an appointment with your careers adviser and discuss all the areas of study you are interested in and the careers which appeal to you. Your adviser will be able to direct you to the information you need. Don't worry if you have to see your adviser many times, and don't be afraid of telling him or her if you don't understand something or want it clarified – they are there to help you!

Talk to your form tutor and any subject teacher you get on well with. They may not have the exact information you need about a specific career, but will be able to show you where to look, or put you in touch with someone who does know.

Go to any career talks your school organises – you might not think they'll interest you, and perhaps they won't, but there is always the chance you will discover an interest in a career you have never thought of before.

When you go to a talk, ask any questions that occur to you, even if you think they sound silly. If you are feeling shy about asking a question in front of all the other pupils, approach the person who is giving the talk at the end of the session. Usually they stay for a while to answer questions on a one-to-one basis.

'A friend of ours was a doctor and for ages I thought I would be one too – until I realised how much maths was involved!'

Becky, now studying history.

Researching careers

A good Internet resource is the careers database on the Connexions Direct website. This groups careers into families, giving you a broad insight into the type of jobs available in any particular area and the qualifications and personal qualities you will need.

The National Careers Helpline also have advisors to talk to between 8am and 2am: contact them on 080 800 132 19 or via the email call back form. You don't have to give personal information and this is a confidential service.

An excellent book to consult is *The Penguin Careers Guide*, which also groups careers in families, listing entry qualifications, work, training and personal attributes. For example, the section on social work has information on careers in field work (including areas such as adoption and child abuse), education welfare work, the probation service and residential care. The section on training outlines the degree route and the postgraduate diploma you can take.

What type of person are you?

Think about the type of person you are and the personal qualities you have – this will help you decide on what careers to aim for. *The Penguin Careers Guide* lists personal attributes needed for each type of work, so it may help to compile a list of adjectives or phrases that you think describe you best. You might like to try this with a friend as well.

Look at the following lists – they are not exhaustive and you can add to them – and mark which ones you think apply to you and which to your friend and then compare notes. You might be quite surprised by the qualities other people see in you!

Are you:

- Artistic?
- Creative?
- Methodical?
- A people person?
- A problem solver?
- An outdoor type?
- Practical?
- Self-motivating?
- Musical?
- Patient?
- Empathetic?

Do you:

- Have the ability to communicate with different types of people?
- Want to make a difference to other people's lives?
- Like working as part of a large team?
- Enjoy working alone?
- Take the initiative?
- Inspire confidence?
- Have good organisational skills?
- Like working with children?

Involving your parents and family

Talk to your parents about what you are considering. Your mum and/or dad know you better than anyone else and may be able to guide you in your choices. Have a chat with grandparents, uncles and aunts and also any brothers, sisters or cousins who have already applied to university – they might have some good tips for you. Members of your family may have friends or work colleagues who can advise you and help you come to a decision.

However, don't be put off something you feel really strongly about by anyone – parents, family, friends or teachers! You will find that almost everyone you know will have an opinion about what you should do. Listen to them politely but don't be bullied into agreeing with them. This is your future!

For example, if you're interested in taking a degree in nursing but your mum says something like, 'You'll never make a nurse, you can't stand the sight of blood!', it may be true that the sight of blood makes you feel faint but you won't be the first person to have to overcome that worry in the medical profession.

Planning work experience

If you want to study medicine, you really should plan your application early, and should start thinking about this as soon as you begin Year 12, if not in Year 11. You will need to show that you have had enough work experience in the field. This will include holiday jobs in a hospital, doing anything from being an orderly to a porter or working in a voluntary capacity. Work experience in medicine is becoming increasingly competitive and some students overcome this by volunteering in health projects abroad. Even before studying the subject, you need to show commitment and stamina.

To study dentistry you need to prove that you have a high level of manual dexterity – that you can do fiddly things with your hands! This could be in anything from cake decoration to model-making. You may also be asked to demonstrate your level of manual dexterity in some way at an interview – so if you are all 'finger and thumbs', dentistry might not be for you.

For law degrees you should have shadowed a solicitor or attended court proceedings (as an observer!). For degrees in media, you will be expected to have visited a radio or television station or be able to show that you have been involved in community media projects. You should also already be involved in your school magazine or website.

For many other careers, your work experience might not be directly relevant but will show that you can work as part of a team, are punctual, personable, a self-starter, good at initiating work and so on.

How to write a CV

You may wonder about the value of writing a CV at this stage in your life, but the purpose is threefold:

1. It will make you recall all the things you have done – not just your academic qualifications but music, gym, swimming, team sports, and any clubs you've attended. This will help you when you come to write your personal statement (see chapter 5) on the UCAS form.

2. You may also want to send a CV (separately) to a university to support the personal statement in your application.

3. You can use it to give to potential employers when you are looking for a Saturday or holiday job.

A CV should include:

- Your name and contact details.
- Date of birth.
- Education to date.
- Any work experience.
- Voluntary work undertaken.
- Non-academic achievements.
- Personal qualities.
- Name and contact details of two people who are not members of your family but know you well who will give you a reference.

Overleaf is the CV Olivia wrote after her A2 results, in order to help her look for a job to finance her gap year travels. She included a photograph (good for helping prospective employers remember you) and received lots of offers of jobs.

Tips for parents

- Keep involved, even if your teenager tries to fob you off.
- Make sure you know all the important dates (see page 9 and Appendix One) and check that your son or daughter is on track.
- If you haven't heard of any meetings at school about university applications, phone them to find out the dates or check the school's website if they have one. Some schools are now initiating an email service to parents, which you can sign up for to keep abreast of what's going on.
- Offer guidance – but be wary of trying to live your life through them.
- Making too strong a case for a particular subject or university can be counterproductive.
- If you went to university yourself, remember that times and institutions have changed.

- Don't feel sidelined if you didn't go to university – you still have a wealth of experience to offer.

- Help with things like organisation and planning – some teenagers are great at this but others really need some firm guidance.

- Be positive – don't belittle a teenager's aspirations. If you think that they are making a mistake, suggest this carefully or offer alternatives for them to think about.

- If things do go wrong in any way, be prepared to visit the school or college to see if matters can be improved.

Olivia Coates	Address
	Telephone number
	Mobile number
	Date of birth
Education:	Sydenham High School
	A Level: Theatre Studies A, Religious Studies A, English B
	GCSE: As: English, English Lit, ICT, Drama, Music, RS
	Bs: French, Maths, Double Science
Duke of Edinburgh:	Bronze, Silver and Gold Awards
General Studies:	B
Young Enterprise:	Merit
School Leaving Prizes:	RS, Theatre Studies, Contribution to School Life
Extracurricular:	Running Drama Club for Year 7
	Peer Mentor
	Drama Prefect
Music Grades:	Singing – grade 4 distinction
	Trumpet – grades 1 to 5
	Piano – grades 1 and 2
University:	Deferred entry
Work Experience:	Journalism – Health and Homeopathy, editorial meetings, proofreading and attended press briefings.
	Babysitting and childcare.
	Waitressing at private parties and paid for events.
	Assistant in St Luke's Primary School, West Norwood.
Voluntary Work:	L'Arche – helping with the mentally and physically disabled.
	Crèche – St John the Evangelist, East Dulwich.
Qualities:	Excellent people skills
	Adaptable
	Friendly
	Reliable
	Honest and hard-working
Referees:	Person one Person two

Summing Up

- Before applying to university you have to consider very carefully about the subjects which interest you and the careers you might be attracted to.

- The more research you do, the better position you will be in to make informed decisions. Your research can be talking to family and friends, consulting teachers at school, and filling in questionnaires like the Stamford Test.

- Think about the type of person you are, the qualities and attributes you have and prepare a CV including all your achievements and relevant experiences.

- Don't put off thinking about your application – the dates for final submission will arrive all too soon!

Chapter Two

Deciding Which Subject to Study

Following on from the last chapter's discussion about the type of career you might like, now you have to think about the subject or subjects you'd like to study to degree level. You should start this at the beginning of Year 12, if not sooner!

It's worth remembering that whatever you decide to study, it will be for the next three or four years, so it must be something you will enjoy. Although some students do manage to swap courses once they have started, this isn't always the case, so you need to be as confident as you can be that the subject you choose is the one for you.

Here are some pointers for you to consider.

Vocational or non-vocational?

A vocational degree is one which leads to a career path – but not necessarily a job straightaway – once you have graduated. You need to have a very clear idea of the career you would like to follow if you choose a vocational degree. Alternatively, you can follow the middle path and opt for a semi-vocational course.

Examples of vocational degrees:

Dentistry, nursing, veterinary, medical, midwifery, teacher training.

Examples of non-vocational degrees:

Philosophy, geography, history, English literature.

Examples of semi-vocational degrees:

Business management, IT, economics, engineering.

Should you opt for a subject you are already familiar with?

If you love a subject and have always been good at it, it's tempting to carry on with it at degree level. There is nothing wrong with this at all and thousands of students make this choice, but it could mean that you are missing out on the opportunity to study a completely new subject. This might be a subject that would be just as appealing, but is something you have never considered. This is why it is important to visit conventions and exhibitions (see page 24).

Another consideration is to link a subject you love and are familiar with, with one you haven't studied before. This can result in you being offered a place at grades you are likely to achieve.

For example, to study English literature you are likely to need three As but if you combine it with philosophy you may only need three Bs.

Choosing a non-vocational course in a subject you are unfamiliar with

This is where it is useful for you to take the Stamford Test on the UCAS website mentioned in the previous chapter, as you can see if your likes and dislikes match up with certain subjects.

You can find out about different types of courses and what they have to offer when you go to a convention or exhibition (see page 24). This is an excellent time to ask questions and read the prospectuses so that you have a better idea of what's involved in studying a particular subject.

UCAS Course Search

The UCAS Course Search lists all the courses in every UK university. You will find this by going to the UCAS website, clicking 'Students' and then the 'Course Search' option.

As an illustration of what's on offer, try this:

* Put in your favourite subject, or the one you enjoy the most, and click 'search'.

* This will give you a comprehensive list of what's on offer.

* Narrow your search by using the drop down menu under 'course type' and/or 'region'.

* From these results choose and write down five new subject ideas that are related to the ones you have most enjoyed studying at AS or IB or BTEC.

Example:

Will keyed in his favourite subject, economics, and chose four regions: East Anglia, East Midlands, West Midlands and Yorkshire.

This produced a list of 436 courses. From quickly scanning the list, Will picked out five subject ideas that he might like to consider: economics and logistics, philosophy, politics and economics, economic/digital media technology, environmental management and international studies with economics.

Competition for university courses

Some subjects are far more in demand than others and so the more popular the course, the more difficult it may be to find a place, and the grades required may be much higher.

Some subjects become more or less popular in particular years. According to figures from UCAS applications for 2011 for all subjects allied to medicine were up 15.3% on the previous year; for subjects including veterinary science/agriculture and related studies the figures show an increase of 11.2% on those for 2010, while applications for creative arts and design were also up by 8.7%.

In the same year, there was a fall in applications for technologies (4.6%), linguistics, classics and related subjects (4%) and combined arts (2.6%).

Most popular courses in 2011:

* Nursing.
* Law.
* Psychology.
* Pre-clinical medicine.

Getting into medical school

Many excellent students fail because there are more applicants than places available. If you are interested in medicine as a career, intensive preparation is needed and you must start early with your work experience and voluntary work.

You must also fulfil some health screening requirements for hepatitis B and immunisation, plus you will need to have a Criminal Records Bureau check. This involves filling out forms and providing proof of your identity and residence.

You might also like to consider these different routes into medicine:

* Five to six-year MB BS or MB ChB course.
* Four-year accelerated graduate entry courses.
* Six-year courses that include a 'pre-med' year.

Visiting conventions and exhibitions

UCAS organises conventions and exhibitions throughout the country. This is where you will be able to meet people from the universities you are interested in, talk about the courses, discover more about their facilities and collect a prospectus and any other information they have to offer.

The conventions begin in March – if you've not heard about one near you, you should ask your teachers for details. You'll find a list of conventions on the UCAS website, just click on your region and all the details will come up. If your school is not organising a visit to a convention during Year 12, you can still attend one on your own and they cost nothing to enter.

Before you go to a convention, however, you need to think about the information you require and the questions you want to ask.

What sort of questions should you ask at conventions?

Attending a convention is a good opportunity to ask about anything you've been concerned about. For instance, you might want to ask if all your A2 subjects are accepted (not all universities recognise every subject) and if you are planning a gap year, is this encouraged?

You should also ask specific questions about the course and what it offers, how many places there are, how many applicants they have each year and whether the university interviews candidates. Then there are more practical considerations you might like to ask about, such as where the student accommodation is in relation to the institution, what the public transport is like and what amenities are available on campus.

Tips for parents

▪ Get your son or daughter to create a spreadsheet, wall chart or calendar so they can mark up important dates to remember. The first will be the days for any conventions and exhibitions held in your area. This will also be a good time to highlight all the important future dates – see Appendix One for the full list.

▪ Keep them focused! It's easy with all the studying they have, to forget or put off thinking about the subject they would like to study at university.

Summing Up

* Deciding what to study is one of the most important decisions you have to make, whether you opt for a vocational or non-vocational course, a subject you are familiar with or something completely new.

* If you haven't already tried the Stamford Test mentioned in the previous chapter, do so now and also follow the course search example (page 22) for yourself.

* Go to any UCAS conventions and exhibitions near you and find out as much as you can about the courses and universities that interest you.

Chapter Three

Choosing Your Universities

When you complete the UCAS form in Year 13, you can choose up to five universities to be considered for, although you don't have to name that many. The institutions will be entered alphabetically, so you don't have to say which is your first choice, and they won't know where else you've applied to.

Before you make your choices though, there are various points you should consider. Again, start thinking about this as soon as you begin Year 12, if not in Year 11!

Choosing where to live

Studying and living at home

In some countries, like France, it has been quite usual for students to attend their nearest university and carry on living at home with their families. Generally, that has not been the custom in the UK, unless there have been particular reasons for doing so – for example, when a student has ill health.

However, with the loss of maintenance grants for the vast majority of students and the introduction of payment for tuition fees, many young people now consider studying and living at home as a more affordable alternative.

Since the academic year beginning in September 2008, the threshold for maintenance grants (see page 94) has been raised and more students will be able to claim, so this consideration may not be so pertinent.

'My eldest daughter based her university choice on the ones nearest to home as I didn't want her to accumulate a huge amount of debt living elsewhere. We've yet to see how it works out.'

Sian, mother of three.

Points to consider if you choose to live at home:

- Will you be able to study effectively – do you have your own room and space?

- Will your parents expect you to be home by certain times – will this affect your social life?

- How independent will you be?

- Will your parents allow you enough freedom to bring friends home when you want to?

- How far will you have to travel each day, and how long will it take?

- Is there a regular bus or will you have to drive?

- How expensive will this be?

'As soon as I got to Exeter, I knew it wasn't for me. I had to be in a big city.'

Ellie, from London and going to study in Leeds.

A big city or a country town?

Some people can't wait to get away from what they are used to. For instance, if you live in a big metropolitan city like Manchester, Birmingham or London you might yearn for the more peaceful setting of Lampeter, or long to be on a campus by the sea, like Sussex. On the other hand, the thought of going somewhere smaller and more provincial might fill you with horror!

Only you know what will suit you best. However, you should not dismiss a university out of hand just because of the location. It may be that although you love big cities, the best place to study the course you've set your heart on is a rural campus, or vice versa.

Campus or central?

Again, this is a matter of what you feel would be better for you. The idea of a campus just outside town with halls of residence and lecture halls within easy walking distance of each other, plus good recreational facilities, is paradise for some students, while others would prefer to be in the heart of the city centre and rubbing shoulders with those who live and work in the area.

Some campuses are a fair distance from the city/town, so you need to consider this when thinking about socialising off-campus. How good is the local transport system?

Distance from home

This may not occur to you at first, but you need to consider how you will get to university and how long it will take you to return home for holidays and the odd weekend. You may also need to think about how much travelling will cost you.

If your family doesn't have a car, you will have to think about how you will get all your possessions to your accommodation. Is this going to be feasible by train if you have to make several changes?

To see a UK map with all the locations of colleges and universities marked, visit www.scit.wlv.ac.uk/ukinfo/.

Viewing universities

Most students, though not all, like to take a look at the universities they are thinking of applying to. Although you can get an idea of the place from the brochures and online facilities, nothing really beats being in a place and seeing it with your own eyes, talking to the students and staff, and finding out what else is on offer.

Open days

You can find out when the open days are for the universities you'd like to visit by going to www.opendays.com. Here you can either use the search facility to look up the open days for specific universities, or click on the calendar to find out which open days are being held on specific dates. You can then click on the university listed for more details.

Most universities have one open day in the summer term and one in the autumn term, some have more. If the summer date is after you have finished exams, this is a good time to go.

Don't try to visit too many universities and don't just go because your friends are going. Make up your own mind about where to visit. You should have been helped in your decision by visiting the conventions and exhibitions (see page 24).

If you are reading this as a Year 11 pupil, you might consider going to a university open day in advance, which will save you time later in Years 12 and 13.

If you miss the open day for a particular university or are unable to attend for some reason, contact the university to find out if there is the possibility of making a visit at another time.

Time off school for viewing

Some schools are quite specific about the amount of time you can take out to view universities – after all, you will be missing lessons and study time that you will have to catch up on. Many open days are on Saturdays – if you can, try to pick these, so it doesn't impinge on your school time.

Student accommodation

While you are viewing a university you are usually offered the opportunity to see the type of student accommodation on offer. If they don't mention this, make sure you ask to see an example of a typical student room.

Some halls are catered – they provide you with breakfast and dinner – and are therefore more expensive. Having your meals provided so that you don't have to budget for food may be appealing, but if you are rarely awake in time for breakfast, or are involved in lots of evening activities, this can just be a waste of money.

Questions you might want to consider about student accommodation:

- Do the halls offer free Internet access?
- What is the price range?
- Is the hall mixed or single sex?

- Do rooms have en suite facilities?

- Do rooms have a hand basin?

- What furniture comes with the room?

- When are the rooms cleaned?

- What are the common rooms like and what is the ratio of students to each kitchen/bathroom/lounge?

- How many weeks are included? (Some halls have students there for 40 weeks but others do not include the Easter break, so you would have to move your belongings out during that vacation.)

In your second year you will probably have to find your own accommodation, so it's worth asking how easy this is, what's on offer and how expensive it tends to be.

Location

Viewing a university puts it into context geographically. A campus which is described as two miles from the city centre might mean you'd have to walk home late at night along unlit country roads because there's no local transport.

Social life

Bars and clubs are found in every town, however it's nice to know what else is on offer. Each student union has its own bars and clubs, but you might like to find out what sort of societies they have as well. For example, you might be interested in music or sport, so it's important to find out what's available. At the open day, visit the union and find out what they offer. Your time at university is a whole experience, not just academic study.

All universities have good points and you need to choose one that matches your own needs. What suits your friends might not be right for you, so make sure you don't make decisions just because that's what your friends are doing. You'll make new friends at university and you'll see your old ones when you return home for holidays.

Do you have special needs?

According to the Higher Education Statistics Agency (HESA), having a disability, learning difficulties or special needs (including dyslexia) should not stop you from studying at university. In fact the numbers of undergraduates with disabilities have been increasing each year from 138,000 in 2006 to 171,305 in 2010.

The Disability Discrimination Act (DDA) means that disabled students must not be discriminated against when they apply to university. The act requires institutions to make 'reasonable adjustments' to their facilities so that disabled students are not at a 'substantial disadvantage'.

Universities and colleges should each have a Disability Equality Scheme which sets out how they plan to increase provision for disabled students so they don't suffer inequalities.

If you have a disability or specific learning difficulty, you should contact the universities you are interested in as soon as possible, and certainly before submitting your application.

You will find that most institutions have disability co-ordinators or advisers. You can look up their contact details on the Skill: National Bureau for Students with Disabilities website at www.skill.org.uk.

You need to know what help is available – the disability co-ordinator can tell you what the support system is like and help set up an information visit. This will give you the chance to find out what adaptations, if any, would be needed if you were to study there.

What you need to find out will vary according to your disability. If there is a charity or organisation linked to your particular disability, they may be able to give you specific information about studying or put you in touch with other students who will be able to give you the benefit of their experience.

A good website to visit is www.direct.gov.uk/en/DisabledPeople.

Visiting university

When you visit a university, prepare a list of facts you need to find out. This might include:

▨ Accessibility of the buildings you need to use.

▨ Facilities for disabled students.

▨ Can you meet any students who have a similar disability?

▨ If you are accepted there who will arrange the support you need?

By informing the university beforehand about your disability, you will give them the opportunity to organise the support you need for the beginning of your course. You may also need to apply for funding through the Disabled Students' Allowances.

These grants, which are not means-tested and do not have to be paid back, are to help with the extra costs you might have because of your disability or specific learning difficulty. This could include paying for things like specialist computer software, a note-taker, a sign language interpreter, Braille paper or extra transport costs.

To find out more and to download DSA forms visit:

England: www.direct.gov.uk/en/EducationAndLearning/ UniversityAndHigherEducation/StudentFinance/index.htm

Wales: www.studentfinancewales.co.uk

Scotland: www.saas.gov.uk

Northern Ireland: www.education-support.org.uk

The cost of travel

▨ If you need to travel by coach or train to visit a university, you should try to book your ticket as far in advance as possible. This way you are much more likely to be able to take advantage of cheap fares.

▨ Apply for a Young Person's Travel Card (you can renew these annually until you are 25) which costs £28 per year and will save you about a third on ticket prices. (When you start university some banks offer a five-year Young Person's Travel Card as an incentive to bank with them.) www.16-25railcard.co.uk/online

* Booking though the Train Line is effective and quick. Remember that if you are travelling on a weekday before 10am your ticket may be more expensive than travelling at a weekend. Very often two single tickets will work out cheaper than one return, and it may be more cost-effective to buy tickets in stages – you won't have to break your journey or the bank! To find out where the train stops en route and to check the prices for each stage, go to the National Rail website or Transport Direct's journey planner.

* If you are going by car, perhaps you or your parent could offer a lift to someone and share the petrol costs.

Comparing universities

The Unistats website (www.unistats.com) is designed to allow you to compare universities and colleges in the UK. It gives you accurate, official and up-to-date information enabling you to:

* Compare UCAS points and other information for different subjects and higher education institutions.

* Find out what recent students have achieved and what sort of jobs they are doing six months after finishing their degree.

* Read what over 220,000 students felt about the quality of their higher education experience in the latest National Student Survey.

Studying in Europe

As many universities in Europe have fees considerably lower than those in the UK, some students are now applying to European universities, many of which teach their courses in English.

If you are thinking about universities in Europe the best place to check out what's available is BachelorsPortal.eu which has the most comprehensive database on first degree courses at universities and schools in Germany, The Netherlands, Belgium, Sweden, Finland, Poland, Spain, France, Italy and 29 other European countries, including the EU (European Union).

The site covers Business, Economics, Social Studies, Natural Sciences, Law, Engineering, Humanities, Environmental Science and all other academic fields.

First, use the search engine to find the degree in your discipline of interest. You will then be presented with your options with a short description, tuition fee (EU and Non-EU), duration and university information. For instance you can study Politics at the University of Luxembourg on a 3-year course at 400 euros per annum taught in English.

Select your preferred study and find all details: application requirements, contents, application deadlines, start dates, mode (full-time, part-time, online/ distance learning), accreditation, scholarship and funding opportunities.

If the programme interests you, you can contact the university directly. You will not be able to claim a student loan for studying in Europe but you may be able to fund this study with a bank loan or help from your family.

Case study

'Money was a factor in choosing Maastricht University — you pay less and you get more teaching time in the Netherlands than you would in the UK.

'We study mostly in tutorials. They are conducted like debates, so you have to do a lot of research and present your arguments well. There are exams every eight weeks and you change subject, tutorial group and tutor each time.

'You have got to pass all of the exams and there's a credit system which means by the end of the year you must have 42 out of 60 to get through to year two.

'It's a cool place to make friends. My only problem so far has been digs. I started off in university accommodation. There is no campus here and it was in an enormous sink estate, soon to be knocked down. The rooms weren't too bad but the area was terrible and it was miles away. I managed to rent a room in a flat with two other students and I'm now about 10 feet from my faculty and right in the middle of town.'

Christian, Maastricht University

Tips for parents

- Check that your son or daughter knows the dates of the open days they want to attend – and tells you when they are! If they are going on their own by train, prompt them to book tickets in advance (see page 33) as they will be cheaper.

- If your son or daughter wants to visit a university without you in tow, make sure you have discussed the type of questions he or she may want to ask and what to look for.

- In the event that you go too, don't take over the day. Let your son or daughter ask the questions and certainly don't answer for them when they are talking to students or lecturers. This is their day!

- If you can avoid it, don't take their siblings along with you. They can be distracting and demanding.

Summing Up

- When you are choosing the universities you want to apply for, you have to consider the type of place you'd feel happy living in, whether you want to be on a campus or in a town or if you would be better off living at home. Open days are a good opportunity for you to assess these questions, as well as finding out about the accommodation on offer.

- If you have a disability or special needs, you need to contact your potential university choices as early as possible to find out the sort of support they offer.

- You should also consider the cost of viewing universities. Bear in mind that your parents may not have lots of spare cash to fund your travelling, and remember you may also be called for interview as well.

Chapter Four

Your UCAS Application

At the end of this chapter you will find the UCAS Tariff charts which show you the points allowed for each examination. Some universities work on the Tariff system and may ask you to achieve, for example, 320 points, while another may ask for ABB. However, it is important to remember that you may also accrue points for achievements like music grades.

You will also find at the end of this book (Appendix Two) a list of the most common terms used by UCAS and what they mean. It is worth reading these carefully so that no misunderstandings arise.

To improve your chance of being offered a place at a university of your choice, you need to submit your application as soon as you can from September onwards and before the 15th January. These dates are the same every year and apply to students in Year 13.

If you are applying to the University of Oxford or University of Cambridge, your application needs to be submitted by the 15th October. This date also applies to those applying for courses in medicine, dentistry and veterinary science or veterinary medicine. These dates are the same every year.

Some art and design courses have a later deadline of the 24th March.

You should check application deadlines for your course on Course Search at www.ucas.com.

In Year 13, when you begin your UCAS application process, your school or college will give you a 'buzzword' so that you can log on to the school system and add to your application as and when you need to.

Your school or college will give you information on how to fill in the UCAS application. You will need to complete your personal information – contact details, whether you have a criminal record, a disability or special needs and your ethnic origin.

There is a separate section on examinations for you to complete, which will include details of the examinations you have taken and the grades achieved, plus the exams you are about to take. Then you have to add the universities you wish to be considered for and write your personal statement (see chapters 5 and 6 for more details on this). You can apply for a maximum of five choices but you don't have to use them all – only add choices you would be happy going to.

Don't worry if you make a mistake – the application can be changed at any time before you actually send it off!

When you have completed your application, your form tutor will add your reference. You will also have to pay a £23 application fee (or £11 if you are only applying to one choice) to UCAS (this will be arranged through your school or college, or you can get a parent to pay by credit or debit card).

Once you have sent in your form, you will be given a unique Personal ID and can log on using this, plus your name and the password you have chosen to track the responses from your chosen universities.

The UCAS application process is evolving all the time. For example, in 2007 the number of universities you could apply to was reduced from six to five, and from 2008 Welsh applicants have been able to apply online in Welsh.

New 'Apply' software on the UCAS site wants to know about:

- Independent study skills.
- Self-awareness.
- Motivation and commitment.
- A realistic understanding of what the course entails.
- Good numeracy and literacy.
- Time management skills.
- Enthusiasm to learn.

Making a good application

When you are completing your UCAS application it's worth thinking about the people who will be reading it and making decisions about you. Most admission tutors are doing this work as well as their 'normal' busy teaching or research work, and they do not receive extra payment. Reading UCAS applications is time-consuming – they are read in batches, and the earliest to arrive are usually read first.

Decisions are made as and when forms are read, so a course can easily be full before the actual deadline is reached. Therefore, you need to present yourself in the best possible light – spelling and grammatical errors could cost you a place. Your past examination results and personal statement are the main indicators that institutions will base their decision upon.

Before sending your application off, you should check again that you fulfil all the requirements and specifications. For example, if you do not have the correct number of GCSE passes at grade C or above, you will be rejected. Make sure you double check the entry requirements for each of the universities you are applying to.

Choosing universities

The previous chapter should have helped you think about how to make your choices. Now, however, there are other points you need to think about.

- You need to consider the grades asked for and the likelihood that you will achieve them. For example, to read English at somewhere like Leeds you will need three As. If this is unlikely, you need to look at a university which demands lower grades for English or combine it with another subject.

- Predicted grades – these are the grades your teachers think you will achieve. Obviously this is not an exact science but teachers are usually very skilled at predicting the grades their students will achieve. It is not in the school's interest to inflate their predictions and you may or may not be told what grades they think you will get.

- Remember that the grades asked for by universities are only a guideline. Edinburgh regularly cites three Bs but in reality offers three As.

'It would have been useful to know about any extracurricular requirements well before the time. I'm thinking here about medicine in particular, but it may apply to other subjects.'

Karen, whose son failed to get into medical school.

- Some universities also require you to take an admission test. For example, UKCAT testing for the UK Clinical Aptitude Test is now a requirement for most UK medical and dental schools. Many law faculties require you to sit the National Admissions Test for Law (LNAT). You should check out whether the institutions you are interested in require you to take a test or present written work. To find out, look at the Entry Profiles on the Course Search at www.ucas.com or contact the universities and colleges direct.

UCAS reference

Your reference is written by your sixth form tutor and should show you in a positive light. It will give a brief character reference, including details of how reliable and punctual you are, plus a short statement about your suitability for the course. It will précis the positive aspects of the reports from each subject teacher and summarise your extracurricular contributions.

You do not see your reference – unless the tutor shows you it.

Applications to the Ruskin School of Drawing & Fine Art, University of Oxford

For this Fine Art course your UCAS application must be made by the 15th October 2011. You must also submit a portfolio of artwork by the 13th November 2011 to the School. You can get more information from the Ruskin School of Drawing & Fine Art, 74 High Street, Oxford, OX1 4BG.

Replying to an offer

Once you have received the decisions from your chosen universities and colleges, you can reply to offers using Track at www.ucas.com. A deadline for your reply will be displayed in Track.

*All dates are correct at the time of going to press, but should be checked by students nearer the time of application. Visit www.ucas.com for confirmation.

UCAS Tariff – which qualifications count for what

This is a points system for achievements for entry into higher education (HE). The Tariff covers different types of qualifications and provides a numerical comparison between applicants. For instance, with this you can work out your points credited for your A2s or International Baccalaureate or your BTEC, plus points given for other examinations like music grades.

The score you end up with does not imply an entitlement to a place on any specific course as other factors are taken into account – including your personal statement, the results of any interview, any entrance tests and your reference.

In July 2010, UCAS announced plans to review the Tariff. This review will take between 18 months and two years. As the review develops, further announcements will be available at www.ucas.com.

The following tables (see overleaf) showing the UCAS Tariff have been reproduced with the kind permission of UCAS.

Tips for parents

※ Make sure you and your son/daughter are aware of the deadline for applications.

※ Discuss the university choices they have made and advise them to check they have, or hope to have, the necessary grades.

The following qualifications are included in the UCAS Tariff. See the number on the qualification title to find the relevant section of the Tariff table.

1   AAT NVQ Level 3 in Accounting
2   AAT Level 3 Diploma in Accounting (QCF)
3   Advanced Diploma
4   Advanced Extension Awards
5   Advanced Placement Programme (US and Canada)
6   Arts Award (Gold)
7   ASDAN Community Volunteering qualification
8   Asset Languages Advanced Stage
9   British Horse Society (Stage 3 Horse Knowledge & Care, Stage 3 Riding and Preliminary Teacher's Certificate)
10 BTEC Awards (NQF)
11 BTEC Certificates and Extended Certificates (NQF)
12 BTEC Diplomas (NQF)
13 BTEC National in Early Years (NQF)
14 BTEC Nationals (NQF)
15 BTEC QCF Qualifications (Suite known as Nationals)
16 BTEC Specialist Qualifications (QCF)
17 CACHE Award, Certificate and Diploma in Child Care and Education
18 CACHE Level 3 Extended Diploma for the Children and Young People's Workforce (QCF)
19 Cambridge ESOL Examinations
20 Cambridge Pre-U
21 Certificate of Personal Effectiveness (COPE)
22 CISI Introduction to Securities and Investment
23 City & Guilds Land Based Services Level 3 Qualifications
24 Graded Dance and Vocational Graded Dance
25 Diploma in Fashion Retail
26 Diploma in Foundation Studies (Art & Design; Art, Design & Media)
27 EDI Level 3 Certificate in Accounting, Certificate in Accounting (IAS)
28 Essential Skills (Northern Ireland)
29 Essential Skills Wales
30 Extended Project (stand alone)
31 Free-standing Mathematics
32 Functional skills
33 GCE (AS, AS Double Award, A level, A level Double Award and A level (with additional AS))
34 Hong Kong Diploma of Secondary Education (from 2012 entry onwards)
35 ifs School of Finance (Certificate and Diploma in Financial Studies)
36 iMedia (OCR level Certificate/Diploma for iMedia Professionals)
37 International Baccalaureate (IB) Diploma
38 International Baccalaureate (IB) Certificate
39 Irish Leaving Certificate (Higher and Ordinary levels)
40 IT Professionals (iPRO) (Certificate and Diploma)
41 Key Skills (Levels 2, 3 and 4)
42 Music examinations (grades 6, 7 and 8)
43 OCR Level 3 Certificate in Mathematics for Engineering
44 OCR Level 3 Certificate for Young Enterprise
45 OCR Nationals (National Certificate, National Diploma and National Extended Diploma)
46 Principal Learning Wales
47 Progression Diploma
48 Rockschool Music Practitioners Qualifications
49 Scottish Qualifications
50 Speech and Drama examinations (grades 6, 7 and 8 and Performance Studies)
51 Sports Leaders UK
52 Welsh Baccalaureate Advanced Diploma (Core)

Updates on the Tariff, including details on the incorporation of any new qualifications, are posted on **www.ucas.com.**

1

AAT NVQ LEVEL 3 IN ACCOUNTING	
GRADE	TARIFF POINTS
PASS	160

2

AAT LEVEL 3 DIPLOMA IN ACCOUNTING	
GRADE	TARIFF POINTS
PASS	160

3

ADVANCED DIPLOMA

Advanced Diploma = Progression Diploma plus Additional & Specialist Learning (ASL). Please see the appropriate qualification to calculate the ASL score. Please see the Progression Diploma (Table 47) for Tariff scores

4

ADVANCED EXTENSION AWARDS	
GRADE	TARIFF POINTS
DISTINCTION	40
MERIT	20

Points for Advanced Extension Awards are over and above those gained from the A level grade

5

ADVANCED PLACEMENT PROGRAMME (US & CANADA)	
GRADE	TARIFF POINTS
Group A	
5	120
4	90
3	60
Group B	
5	50
4	35
3	20

Details of the subjects covered by each group can be found at www.ucas.com/students/ucas_tariff/tarifftables

6

ARTS AWARD (GOLD)	
GRADE	TARIFF POINTS
PASS	35

7

ASDAN COMMUNITY VOLUNTEERING QUALIFICATION	
GRADE	TARIFF POINTS
CERTIFICATE	50
AWARD	30

8

ASSET LANGUAGES ADVANCED STAGE			
GRADE	TARIFF POINTS	GRADE	TARIFF POINTS
Speaking		Listening	
GRADE 12	28	GRADE 12	25
GRADE 11	20	GRADE 11	18
GRADE 10	12	GRADE 10	11
Reading		Writing	
GRADE 12	25	GRADE 12	25
GRADE 11	18	GRADE 11	18
GRADE 10	11	GRADE 10	11

9

BRITISH HORSE SOCIETY	
GRADE	TARIFF POINTS
Stage 3 Horse Knowledge & Care	
PASS	35
Stage 3 Riding	
PASS	35
Preliminary Teacher's Certificate	
PASS	35

Awarded by Equestrian Qualifications (GB) Ltd (EQL)

10

BTEC AWARDS (NQF) (EXCLUDING BTEC NATIONAL QUALIFICATIONS)			
GRADE	TARIFF POINTS		
	Group A	Group B	Group C
DISTINCTION	20	30	40
MERIT	13	20	26
PASS	7	10	13

Details of the subjects covered by each group can be found at www.ucas.com/students/ucas_tariff/tarifftables

11

BTEC CERTIFICATES AND EXTENDED CERTIFICATES (NQF) (EXCLUDING BTEC NATIONAL QUALIFICATIONS)					
GRADE	TARIFF POINTS				
	Group A	Group B	Group C	Group D	Extended Certificates
DISTINCTION	40	60	80	100	60
MERIT	26	40	52	65	40
PASS	13	20	26	35	20

Details of the subjects covered by each group can be found at www.ucas.com/students/ucas_tariff/tarifftables

12

BTEC DIPLOMAS (NQF) (EXCLUDING BTEC NATIONAL QUALIFICATIONS)			
GRADE	TARIFF POINTS		
	Group A	Group B	Group C
DISTINCTION	80	100	120
MERIT	52	65	80
PASS	26	35	40

Details of the subjects covered by each group can be found at www.ucas.com/students/ucas_tariff/tarifftables

13

BTEC NATIONAL IN EARLY YEARS (NQF)					
GRADE	TARIFF POINTS	GRADE	TARIFF POINTS	GRADE	TARIFF POINTS
Theory				Practical	
Diploma		Certificate		D	120
DDD	320	DD	200	M	80
DDM	280	DM	160	P	40
DMM	240	MM	120		
MMM	220	MP	80		
MMP	160	PP	40		
MPP	120				
PPP	80				

Points apply to the following qualifications only: BTEC National Diploma in Early Years (100/1279/5); BTEC National Certificate in Early Years (100/1280/1)

14

BTEC NATIONALS (NQF)					
GRADE	TARIFF POINTS	GRADE	TARIFF POINTS	GRADE	TARIFF POINTS
Diploma		Certificate		Award	
DDD	360	DD	240	D	120
DDM	320	DM	200	M	80
DMM	280	MM	160	P	40
MMM	240	MP	120		
MMP	200	PP	80		
MPP	160				
PPP	120				

15

BTEC QUALIFICATIONS (QCF) (SUITE OF QUALIFICATIONS KNOWN AS NATIONALS)					
EXTENDED DIPLOMA	DIPLOMA	90 CREDIT DIPLOMA	SUBSIDIARY DIPLOMA	CERTIFICATE	TARIFF POINTS
D*D*D*					420
D*D*D					400
D*DD					380
DDD					360
DDM					320
DMM	D*D*				280
	D*D				260
MMM	DD				240
		D*D*			210
MMP	DM	D*D			200
		DD			180
MPP	MM	DM			160
			D*		140
PPP	MP	MM	D		120
		MP			100
	PP		M		80
			D*		70
		PP	D		60
			P	M	40
				P	20

16

BTEC SPECIALIST (QCF)			
GRADE	TARIFF POINTS		
	Diploma	Certificate	Award
DISTINCTION	120	60	20
MERIT	80	40	13
PASS	40	20	7

Need2Know

17

CACHE LEVEL 3 AWARD, CERTIFICATE AND DIPLOMA IN CHILD CARE & EDUCATION					
AWARD		CERTIFICATE		DIPLOMA	
GRADE	TARIFF POINTS	GRADE	TARIFF POINTS	GRADE	TARIFF POINTS
A	30	A	110	A	360
B	25	B	90	B	300
C	20	C	70	C	240
D	15	D	55	D	180
E	10	E	35	E	120

18

CACHE LEVEL 3 EXTENDED DIPLOMA FOR THE CHILDREN AND YOUNG PEOPLE'S WORKFORCE (QCF)	
GRADE	TARIFF POINTS
A*	420
A	340
B	290
C	240
D	140
E	80

19

CAMBRIDGE ESOL EXAMINATIONS	
GRADE	TARIFF POINTS
Certificate of Proficiency in English	
A	140
B	110
C	70
Certificate in Advanced English	
A	70

20

CAMBRIDGE PRE-U					
GRADE	TARIFF POINTS	GRADE	TARIFF POINTS	GRADE	TARIFF POINTS
Principal Subject		Global Perspectives and Research		Short Course	
D1	TBC	D1	TBC	D1	TBC
D2	145	D2	140	D2	TBC
D3	130	D3	126	D3	60
M1	115	M1	112	M1	53
M2	101	M2	98	M2	46
M3	87	M3	84	M3	39
P1	73	P1	70	P1	32
P2	59	P2	56	P2	26
P3	46	P3	42	P3	20

21

CERTIFICATE OF PERSONAL EFFECTIVENESS (COPE)	
GRADE	TARIFF POINTS
PASS	70

Points are awarded for the Certificate of Personal Effectiveness (CoPE) awarded by ASDAN and CCEA

22

CISI INTRODUCTION TO SECURITIES AND INVESTMENT	
GRADE	TARIFF POINTS
PASS WITH DISTINCTION	60
PASS WITH MERIT	40
PASS	20

23

CITY AND GUILDS LAND BASED SERVICES LEVEL 3 QUALIFICATIONS				
GRADE	TARIFF POINTS			
	EXTENDED DIPLOMA	DIPLOMA	SUBSIDIARY DIPLOMA	CERTIFICATE
DISTINCTION*	420	280	140	70
DISTINCTION	360	240	120	60
MERIT	240	160	80	40
PASS	120	80	40	20

24

GRADED DANCE AND VOCATIONAL GRADED DANCE					
GRADE	TARIFF POINTS	GRADE	TARIFF POINTS	GRADE	TARIFF POINTS
Graded Dance					
Grade 8		Grade 7		Grade 6	
DISTINCTION	65	DISTINCTION	55	DISTINCTION	40
MERIT	55	MERIT	45	MERIT	35
PASS	45	PASS	35	PASS	30
Vocational Graded Dance					
Advanced Foundation		Intermediate			
DISTINCTION	70	DISTINCTION	65		
MERIT	55	MERIT	50		
PASS	45	PASS	40		

25

DIPLOMA IN FASHION RETAIL	
GRADE	TARIFF POINTS
DISTINCTION	160
MERIT	120
PASS	80

Applies to the NQF and QCF versions of the qualifications awarded by ABC Awards

26

DIPLOMA IN FOUNDATION STUDIES (ART & DESIGN AND ART, DESIGN & MEDIA)	
GRADE	TARIFF POINTS
DISTINCTION	285
MERIT	225
PASS	165

Awarded by ABC, Edexcel, UAL and WJEC

27

EDI LEVEL 3 CERTIFICATE IN ACCOUNTING, CERTIFICATE IN ACCOUNTING (IAS)	
GRADE	TARIFF POINTS
DISTINCTION	120
MERIT	90
PASS	70

28

ESSENTIAL SKILLS (NORTHERN IRELAND)	
GRADE	TARIFF POINTS
LEVEL 2	10

Only allocated at level 2 if studied as part of a wider composite qualification such as 14-19 Diploma or Welsh Baccalaureate

29

ESSENTIAL SKILLS WALES	
GRADE	TARIFF POINTS
LEVEL 4	30
LEVEL 3	20
LEVEL 2	10

Only allocated at level 2 if studied as part of a wider composite qualification such as 14-19 Diploma or Welsh Baccalaureate

30

EXTENDED PROJECT (STAND ALONE)	
GRADE	TARIFF POINTS
A*	70
A	60
B	50
C	40
D	30
E	20

Points for the Extended Project cannot be counted if taken as part of Progression/Advanced Diploma

31

FREE-STANDING MATHEMATICS	
GRADE	TARIFF POINTS
A	20
B	17
C	13
D	10
E	7

Covers free-standing Mathematics - Additional Maths, Using and Applying Statistics, Working with Algebraic and Graphical Techniques, Modelling with Calculus

32

FUNCTIONAL SKILLS	
GRADE	TARIFF POINTS
LEVEL 2	10

Only allocated if studied as part of a wider composite qualification such as 14-19 Diploma or Welsh Baccalaureate

33

GCE AND VCE									
GRADE	TARIFF POINTS	GRADE	TARIFF POINTS	GRADE	TARIFF POINTS	GRADE	TARIFF POINTS	GRADE	TARIFF POINTS
GCE & AVCE Double Award		GCE A level with additional AS (9 units)		GCE A level & AVCE		GCE AS Double Award		GCE AS & AS VCE	
A*A*	280	A*A	200	A*	140	AA	120	A	60
A*A	260	AA	180	A	120	AB	110	B	50
AA	240	AB	170	B	100	BB	100	C	40
AB	220	BB	150	C	80	BC	90	D	30
BB	200	BC	140	D	60	CC	80	E	20
BC	180	CC	120	E	40	CD	70		
CC	160	CD	110			DD	60		
CD	140	DD	90			DE	50		
DD	120	DE	80			EE	40		
DE	100	EE	60						
EE	80								

34

HONG KONG DIPLOMA OF SECONDARY EDUCATION					
GRADE	TARIFF POINTS	GRADE	TARIFF POINTS	GRADE	TARIFF POINTS
All subjects except mathematics		Mathematics compulsory component		Mathematics optional components	
5**	No value	5**	No value	5**	No value
5*	130	5*	60	5*	70
5	120	5	45	5	60
4	80	4	35	4	50
3	40	3	25	3	40

No value for 5** pending receipt of candidate evidence (post 2012)

35

IFS SCHOOL OF FINANCE (NQF & QCF)			
GRADE	TARIFF POINTS	GRADE	TARIFF POINTS
Certificate in Financial Studies (CeFS)		Diploma in Financial Studies (DipFS)	
A	60	A	120
B	50	B	100
C	40	C	80
D	30	D	60
E	20	E	40

Applicants with the ifs Diploma cannot also count points allocated to the ifs Certificate. Completion of both qualifications will result in a maximum of 120 UCAS Tariff points

36

LEVEL 3 CERTIFICATE / DIPLOMA FOR iMEDIA USERS (iMEDIA)	
GRADE	TARIFF POINTS
DIPLOMA	66
CERTIFICATE	40

Awarded by OCR

37

INTERNATIONAL BACCALAUREATE (IB) DIPLOMA			
GRADE	TARIFF POINTS	GRADE	TARIFF POINTS
45	720	34	479
44	698	33	457
43	676	32	435
42	654	31	413
41	632	30	392
40	611	29	370
39	589	28	348
38	567	27	326
37	545	26	304
36	523	25	282
35	501	24	260

38

INTERNATIONAL BACCALAUREATE (IB) CERTIFICATE					
GRADE	TARIFF POINTS	GRADE	TARIFF POINTS	GRADE	TARIFF POINTS
Higher Level		Standard Level		Core	
7	130	7	70	3	120
6	110	6	59	2	80
5	80	5	43	1	40
4	50	4	27	0	10
3	20	3	11		

39

IRISH LEAVING CERTIFICATE			
GRADE	TARIFF POINTS	GRADE	TARIFF POINTS
Higher		Ordinary	
A1	90	A1	39
A2	77	A2	26
B1	71	B1	20
B2	64	B2	14
B3	58	B3	7
C1	52		
C2	45		
C3	39		
D1	33		
D2	26		
D3	20		

40

IT PROFESSIONALS (iPRO)	
GRADE	TARIFF POINTS
DIPLOMA	100
CERTIFICATE	80

Awarded by OCR

41

KEY SKILLS	
GRADE	TARIFF POINTS
LEVEL 4	30
LEVEL 3	20
LEVEL 2	10

Only allocated at level 2 if studied as part of a wider composite qualification such as 14-19 Diploma or Welsh Baccalaureate

42

MUSIC EXAMINATIONS								
GRADE	TARIFF POINTS		GRADE	TARIFF POINTS		GRADE	TARIFF POINTS
Practical								
Grade 8			Grade 7			Grade 6		
DISTINCTION	75		DISTINCTION	60		DISTINCTION	45
MERIT	70		MERIT	55		MERIT	40
PASS	55		PASS	40		PASS	25
Theory								
Grade 8			Grade 7			Grade 6		
DISTINCTION	30		DISTINCTION	20		DISTINCTION	15
MERIT	25		MERIT	15		MERIT	10
PASS	20		PASS	10		PASS	5

Points shown are for the ABRSM, LCMM/University of West London, Rockschool and Trinity Guildhall/Trinity College London Advanced Level music examinations

43

OCR LEVEL 3 CERTIFICATE IN MATHEMATICS FOR ENGINEERING	
GRADE	TARIFF POINTS
A*	TBC
A	90
B	75
C	60
D	45
E	30

44

OCR LEVEL 3 CERTIFICATE FOR YOUNG ENTERPRISE	
GRADE	TARIFF POINTS
DISTINCTION	40
MERIT	30
PASS	20

45

OCR NATIONALS								
GRADE	TARIFF POINTS		GRADE	TARIFF POINTS		GRADE	TARIFF POINTS
National Extended Diploma			National Diploma			National Certificate		
D1	360		D	240		D	120
D2/M1	320		M1	200		M	80
M2	280		M2/P1	160		P	40
M3	240		P2	120			
P1	200		P3	80			
P2	160						
P3	120						

46

PRINCIPAL LEARNING WALES	
GRADE	TARIFF POINTS
A*	210
A	180
B	150
C	120
D	90
E	60

47

PROGRESSION DIPLOMA	
GRADE	TARIFF POINTS
A*	350
A	300
B	250
C	200
D	150
E	100

Advanced Diploma = Progression Diploma plus Additional & Specialist Learning (ASL). Please see the appropriate qualification to calculate the ASL score

48

GRADE	ROCKSCHOOL MUSIC PRACTITIONERS QUALIFICATIONS				
	TARIFF POINTS				
	Extended Diploma	Diploma	Subsidiary Diploma	Extended Certificate	Certificate
DISTINCTION	240	180	120	60	30
MERIT	160	120	80	40	20
PASS	80	60	40	20	10

49

SCOTTISH QUALIFICATIONS							
GRADE	TARIFF POINTS	GRADE	TARIFF POINTS	GRADE	TARIFF POINTS	GROUP	TARIFF POINTS
Advanced Higher		Higher		Scottish Interdisciplinary Project		Scottish National Certificates	
A	130	A	80	A	65	C	125
B	110	B	65	B	55	B	100
C	90	C	50	C	45	A	75
D	72	D	36				
Ungraded Higher		NPA PC Passport					
PASS	45	PASS	45				
		Core Skills					
		HIGHER	20				

Details of the subjects covered by each Scottish National Certificate can be found at www.ucas.com/students/ucas_tariff/tarifftables

50

SPEECH AND DRAMA EXAMINATIONS							
GRADE	TARIFF POINTS	GRADE	TARIFF POINTS	GRADE	TARIFF POINTS	GRADE	TARIFF POINTS
PCertLAM		Grade 8		Grade 7		Grade 6	
DISTINCTION	90	DISTINCTION	65	DISTINCTION	55	DISTINCTION	40
MERIT	80	MERIT	60	MERIT	50	MERIT	35
PASS	60	PASS	45	PASS	35	PASS	20

Details of the Speech and Drama Qualifications covered by the Tariff can be found at www.ucas.com/students/ucas_tariff/tarifftables

51

SPORTS LEADERS UK	
GRADE	TARIFF POINTS
PASS	30

These points are awarded to Higher Sports Leader Award and Level 3 Certificate in Higher Sports Leadership (QCF)

52

WELSH BACCALAUREATE ADVANCED DIPLOMA (CORE)	
GRADE	TARIFF POINTS
PASS	120

These points are awarded only when a candidate achieves the Welsh Baccalaureate Advanced Diploma

Summing Up

▓ Once you have the school or college 'buzzword', you can access your application form at any time by logging on to the school system. The information you give about yourself must be accurate and truthful.

▓ Be especially careful about spelling and grammar as errors could mean you won't be offered a place.

▓ For art and design you must be able to present a portfolio of your work.

Chapter Five

Writing Your
Personal Statement

The personal statement on your UCAS application is so important that two whole chapters are devoted to just that! It is vital to get it right and on no account should it be left to the last moment. In fact, start writing it now – if you haven't already begun. The worst thing you can do is ignore it and then find you have to produce it in a rush when you may have coursework due as well.

Once you have completed your statement online, it then goes to your school or college referee who checks your application for accuracy and writes their report.

If you are applying after you have left full-time education, you must paste in your reference and then submit the application yourself.

Your personal statement is your chance to present yourself to the admissions tutors as a rounded character. For most university courses, you will not be invited to an interview, so this is your only chance to 'speak directly' to the admissions department. Therefore, make sure you make the best use of this space – it may gain or lose you a place!

Your personality should 'shine through' a personal statement, so ensure it mentions your passions, enthusiasms, interests, career aspirations (however vague they are) and hobbies. You can also mention current affairs, particularly if they are relevant to your degree choice and any voluntary work you have undertaken.

Length

You are allowed up to 4,000 characters (these include spaces between words) or 47 lines of text, including any blank lines. You do not need to use all of the space allocated, but you won't be allowed to write any more than this.

You should prepare your personal statement offline using a word-processing package which allows you to see the number of characters, words and lines used. Once you are satisfied with your personal statement, paste it into the 'Apply' system and remember to save it!

Drafting (one)

You may find that you need to draft and rewrite your personal statement several times before you have a finished version you are happy with. Don't worry about this, but start working on your statement as early as you can. Many pupils take time during the summer holidays between Years 12 and 13 to start thinking and composing. This is an excellent thing to do!

When you first start writing, don't worry about length or style, just concentrate on getting everything down that you want to say. You can think about editing and perfecting your statement at a later stage.

What to include in your personal statement:

- Say why you have chosen the course(s) you have listed. Each university on your application form will see the personal statement, even though they cannot see your other choices.

- Mention what interests you about the subject you have chosen to study and why.

- If you can link this into any career plans you have, do so.

- Include details of any jobs, work experience or volunteering you have completed. Don't forget to mention the skills and experience you have gained, especially if this is relevant to your subject.

- If you have participated in summer schools or mentoring activities, say so.

- If you have taken part in master classes or other gifted and talented programmes, including those offered by the National Academy for Gifted and Talented Youth (NAGTY), mention them.

- Give details of any skills you have that are not included in the UCAS Tariff (see chapter 4), for example, music grades 1-5, Duke of Edinburgh's Award scheme, Young Enterprise, the army, navy and air force cadet schemes, Liverpool Enrichment Programme.

- If you have applied for any sponsorships or placements, mention them.

- If you are planning to take a 'gap year' (deferred entry, see chapter 7) give your reasons why and say what you are going to do.

- Include what you like to do in your spare time and mention any future plans you have.

Seeking advice and help

Once you have a draft version of your personal statement, print it out and read it through – it's amazing just how many mistakes anyone can miss when reading a document on screen! Ask your parents to read it too; they may have helpful comments and may also remember something you have forgotten to mention.

Your teachers may ask to see your statement and offer their comments, and you can ask other people to give you their opinions. But remember this is your personal statement and you have the last word.

Whatever you do, please do not go to websites that advertise personal statements – your statement will be run through software, which checks for plagiarism. See the tips on page 57 for more information on this.

Drafting (two)

When everyone has made their suggestions, key them in on your copy in a different colour and save as another file. Print this one out and carefully consider the changes you want to incorporate and those you don't like or want.

Make the changes you think are appropriate and then save as another file. (It's a good idea to keep each of your drafts in case you want to revert to an earlier version.)

Check the number of characters and lines (this is easy to do in Word). By this time, your personal statement is more than likely way over the allocated 4,000 characters. Don't panic – now is the time for pruning and fine-tuning.

Again, the next stage is probably better done on a printed version, but if you want to do it on screen make sure you save it as another file, just in case you change your mind. Watch out for repetitions and long-winded phrases that could be shortened.

Look at the following sentence: 'I think that I have good people skills'. This could be reduced to 'I have good people skills' – and you will have saved 13 characters!

Make punctuation work for you. Think of using a semi-colon instead of 'and' and brackets, where appropriate.

Olivia applied to university to study drama after she had her A2 results because she had withdrawn her first application when she realised she had made the wrong choice of subject. Opposite is her personal statement showing the way she amended and shortened it. The words in square brackets are additions. This example will give you ideas and help you to work on your own personal statement.

Important points to remember

- Don't use text language or inappropriate language as this will definitely count against you.

- Do not rely on a spellcheck – they do not pick up differences between, for instance: their and there. Some will have US rather than UK spellings.

- Don't show off or give the impression of arrogance – you need to write about your achievements positively without hyperbole.

- You must be truthful and accurate, don't lie about something – you could easily be caught out at interview.

- For the same reason, don't exaggerate your achievements – you may be asked to show proof of what you have done.

- Don't get a parent/adviser to complete your personal statement – admissions tutors can tell.

- Above all, do not plagiarise. This is copying a personal statement from anyone else or a website. Your personal statement should be your own work. UCAS checks identity and academic qualifications, and uses software applications to detect plagiarism. If they think you have copied your statement, all the universities and colleges to which you have applied to will be informed. They will then take the action they consider to be appropriate. UCAS will also contact you by email.

Tips for parents

- You may have to nag your son or daughter to write their personal statement. Encourage them to write it as early as possible.

- Do not be tempted to write the statement for them – admissions tutors spot an adult's work a mile off!

~~I have chosen to study~~ Drama [became my passion] at ~~university. I first became strongly interested in drama at~~ the age of seven, when I was desperate to be Angel Gabriel in our nativity play! ~~This part I was granted~~ [I passed the audition] and from the moment I stepped on to the stage I knew ~~I had a passion for~~ acting [was for me]. My Year 6 leavers' production was *Bugsy Malone* ~~– one of my all-time favourites – in which~~ I played Tallulah. Not only did I have to act and dance but had to sing as well, and I realised then that I had a real aptitude for performing. My newly discovered voice enabled me to ~~not only~~ take part in numerous concerts singing ~~in the school choir and also doing~~ duets and solo ~~performances~~.

~~Since then~~ I have been in numerous school productions playing leading roles, as well as Assistant Director and Co-Producer. In the latter role I raised £380, ~~which~~ enabl~~ed~~[ing] us to hire the tiered seating necessary for our production of *Alice*. This required real commitment: ~~as~~ I had to give up most weeknights for the rehearsals and ~~all~~ weekends for fundraising. Not only did I have to be very confident, professional and organised, which required great stamina, I also had to work with other people, many of who were my ~~age~~ [peers] ~~and good friends of mine~~, which made it difficult when having to ~~tell~~[instruct] them ~~what to do~~ or tell them off for a lack of punctuality. But ~~I always tried my hardest to use~~ my experience in teamwork and my compassionate nature ~~to~~ aid[ed] me ~~in my role~~.

~~From an early age I have attended the theatre, seeing not only major West End productions but also works in progress and repertory productions.~~

~~I have taken both GCSE and AS level drama and am continuing into A2 this year~~.

[With each of my A level subjects I have developed my analytical and essay writing skills, and learned how to interpret documents, how to construct arguments or debates, develop teamwork skills, confidence and understanding into other people's points of view and ways of life. I have been consistently hard-working, especially in Theatre Studies and Religious Studies, where I was top of the class.

At the end of last year I was awarded three school prizes: Drama, Religious Studies and Commitment to School Life.]

Last year I was elected Drama Prefect ~~for my commitment to the subject,~~ and this has spurred me on to new and exciting ideas, especially for the Inter House Drama Competitions and Drama Festivals, both of which I had huge involvement in. I also ran the Year 7 drama club~~, which not only allows them to experiment with new ideas but it also gives me the opportunity to offer advice and guidance where necessary~~.

My work experience was at St Luke's Primary School, where, as a classroom assistant, I worked mainly with children with special needs and learning difficulties. This was very challenging, however thoroughly rewarding as the children were so responsive ~~and full of energy~~.

During the summer of 2006 I volunteered at L'Arche Lambeth, a Christian community which works to improve the lives of the disabled. ~~They have five houses in the community, and~~ For one week I lived ~~in one~~ there and continue to offer support on a regular basis. This was both mentally and physically demanding, but enjoyable and has made me think of a career in ~~which I can use~~ drama ~~as~~ therapy. ~~As I am a perfectionist I aspire to do this in the best possible way.~~

Fundraising for our local church was something I became involved with through my mother, as she was chief fundraiser. ~~We put on many events, a~~ As well as seeking sponsorship from local businesses [we held many events]~~. The events~~ included[ing] a play in which I had a role, which was produced and directed by professionals~~, and I also helped publicise this. Thus highlighting my eagerness to be involved in all aspects of this subject~~.

I have taken ~~several~~ music examinations, ~~including~~ trumpet: grades ~~one~~ 1 to ~~five~~ 5 – two of which were Merit; piano: grades ~~one~~1 and ~~two~~ 2 and singing: grade 4 ~~four with~~ distinction. [I play] ~~T~~the trumpet ~~is the instrument that I play~~ most frequently, especially in church services and at ~~two~~ weddings. I was also a guest soloist in a concert and have played solos and in the orchestra in many school concerts.

~~I babysit on a regular basis. I not only have to be responsible for these children but I often have to feed and bath them and then put them to bed. This, along with schoolwork, can be very hard work, however I like to be organised and professional, and pride myself in meeting deadlines. During the past two years I have been childminding during the summer, looking after up to three children. This is very challenging, but I enjoy planning interesting activities for them. I also~~ have helped out in a crèche and attended a first aid course tending to both adults and children, as part of my Duke of Edinburgh community service [and]

~~Duke of Edinburgh is something which I started at the age of thirteen and have completed this year.~~ I have gained Bronze, Silver and Gold Awards. I had to learn to work in a team, ~~as this was not rewarding you on your personal skills, but your ability to work with others and plan in advance, which shows I am multitalented. I had to learn~~ to map read and use a compass which is extremely difficult, but with my persistence I managed it. ~~This was~~ [The expeditions were] physically challenging, however it shows I have strong commitment and will strive in difficult situations~~, highlighting that I am not somebody who gives up easily~~. I have taken my Young Enterprise (merit), which I feel has strengthened my public speaking and group work, enabling me, for the first time, to really see what can come from hard work.

~~In my GCSE's I achieved six As and four Bs and in my AS Levels I got an A, two Bs, a C and a D. I studied Theatre Studies; in which I received my A, English, Religious Studies and Sociology. This year I decided to drop sociology and concentrate on the three other subjects, which have most interested me. With each of these subjects I have developed my analytical and essay writing skills, and learned how to interpret documents, how to construct arguments or debates, teamwork skills, confidence and understanding into other people's points of view and ways of life. I have been consistent in my work in all subjects, especially in Religious Studies, where I am top of the class.~~

I am [taking] ~~applying for deferred entry to university as I plan to take~~ a gap year, ~~. Apart from~~ travelling to ~~places like~~ Asia, Australia and Singapore. I ~~will be partaking in at least one voluntary service overseas. In Ghana I~~ [also] plan to ~~work in an orphanage and teach English and hopefully do the same in Romania. I feel this will not only be rewarding to me but especially to the children involved.~~ [volunteer with NGOs whilst travelling.]

My career aspirations are either directing or drama therapy, [however I would love to gain experience acting in the theatre].

Summing Up

- Writing your personal statement is the most important part of your UCAS application. It can be hard work but you must devote enough time for it to be a true reflection of your achievements, attributes and personality.

- Read through this chapter again and take note of all the important points to remember. If you put your mind to it, you will be able to produce a statement that makes admissions tutors look on you favourably, even if your previous examination results are not as high as you would have hoped.

Chapter Six

Examples of Personal Statements

The following personal statements are reproduced exactly as they were entered onto the UCAS form. These three students represent different types of application: vocational, academic and art and design.

This is the personal statement from Gerard who decided, after taking his AS exams, that A levels were not for him. He enrolled at college to take the Key Skills qualifications in Application of Number, Communication and Information Technology, and was studying for a BTEC National Diploma in Public Services (Uniformed) when he applied to university.

'I have been interested in outdoor activities since my first school activity trip to a PGL camp. It has become a passion through taking many walking trips across Britain and France. I would like to take the degree course in order to learn more activity skills and increase my knowledge of the outdoor activities industry, to prepare me for a career in outdoor activities tutoring or management, preferably working with young people in the more adventurous activities.

'My studies on the BTEC National Diploma in Public Services have enabled me to further my interests in sports such as rock climbing, kayaking and mountaineering. During my two year course my studies have included Adventurous Activities, Teamwork, Diversity, Leadership and Expedition Skills. These, along with others I have studied as part of my course, have given me a good foundation for a degree course in outdoor activities and adventure recreation.

'My AS results weren't very good. But I had a phone call from Sheffield to invite me for an interview because they liked my personal statement.'

Mark, studying computer science and artificial intelligence.

'Gap years must be well structured for you to get the most benefit from them – they are not an excuse to laze around and do nothing!'

'Whilst at Bedford College I have also done several extra curricular activities. I have been on many mountaineering trips across Britain where I have learnt first-hand about skills such as map reading, leadership and bushcraft. In the near future, I will also be organising and leading such a trip to the Peak District.

'In addition to the mountaineering trips with college, I have been on many climbing trips, from the crags in the Lake District to Peterborough's climbing wall, including one trip which, as part of one of our core units at college, I co-organised. This involved completing a risk assessment and organising travel.

'This summer, I put what I had learnt into practice, rescuing someone with a broken foot and (with a fellow student) carrying him most of the way down Snowdon until he could be assessed by the rangers.

'I will be studying for the Level Two Awards for Basic Expedition Leader, run by Sports UK, before I leave college. College also offers an Enrichment Scheme, involving weekly rock climbing or kayaking and canoeing which I enjoy taking part in and working towards my BCU 1 star qualification in kayaking.

'One of the proudest moments of my life is being chosen to represent my college in Skills Challenge Day. When representatives of colleges from around the country came to Bedford College to compete in team activities, which included challenges from the police, fire service, ambulance and one of raft building, my team came second.

'From my work experience position as an assistant for Harriet Harman, MP for Peckham in the House of Commons, I developed people skills by answering the phone and dealing with members of the public who were upset or angry.

'I have also developed skills at Poplars Garden Centre where for the past two years I have worked at weekends, assisting customers and generally helping out with the running of the garden centre. My voluntary work clearing scrubland and surveying river pollution with North Chilterns Trust has given me concrete evidence of the value of land management and conservation. I have also assisted with classes for teenagers with learning disabilities.

'Outside college, I am very much an outdoors person; living on a smallholding I am used to being outdoors in all weathers and looking after the animals. I also go beating for a local pheasant shoot (in season).

'During the summer of 2007 I studied to become a qualified lifeguard, learning a great deal from rescue techniques to first aid and gaining a National Pool Lifeguard Qualification. I am a sociable person and enjoy mountain biking with friends.

'The outdoor life is very important to me and I am very excited about studying on an outdoor activities course at university. I know that I have the academic strength, knowledge, stamina, people skills and commitment to undertake the course and to use it to pursue a career in outdoor activities management.'

Lucy was taking A2s in biology, physics, maths and economics. Her personal statement explains why she is interested in neuro-sciences, the subject she has applied to study, and all bar one of her choices are in London, her home city.

'Due to important events in my life I have decided that I would like to pursue a career as a researcher in the field of science. Perhaps the most significant of these was my mother's meningiona in 2000. She was admitted to Kings for an emergency craniotomy and I spent much of that summer visiting her and trying to help around the wards (as much as a 10-year-old could!).

'In 2003, my mum had gamma-knife surgery. A bit older, and a bit more aware, I was fascinated by the fact that non-invasive treatment was available and was surprised by the similarities between the MRI scanner and the gamma knife. This experience made me aware of not only the medical side but also the patients' viewpoint in such situations.

'Last year I enjoyed my work placement where I worked with older people suffering from dementia. Although slightly nervous at first, I found it easy to talk to and relate to the clients during activities such as the art and music classes. It made me realise that, although affected by the same disease, people's reactions and symptoms can vary considerably. This altered my opinions on subjects, such as the area of human robotics, as I realised that designing a care-bot for unpredictable patients would be challenging and costly.

'This year I have done five subjects at AS Level. I chose these with an eye to my future. Economics, in particular, has not only created much more variety in my studies, but also opened my eyes to the importance of cost-efficiency, especially in fast growing areas such as bioengineering and healthcare.

'I have enjoyed many aspects of my subjects this year, in particular the health and disease module in biology and a physics trip to the radiology department of Kings. We observed CT and MRI scanning, X rays and ultrasound – I even got to take home an ultrasound image of my carotid artery!

'I am looking forward to several aspects of A2, especially the two optional modules in biology and physics. These are mammalian physiology and behaviour and medical physics. I am pleased that the syllabus is catering so closely to my interests.

'Outside of school, I have been learning Japanese for two years. I am currently reading a book by Haruki Murakami about 'Tokyo Gas Attacks and the Japanese Psyche'. He constructs this book by taking interviews of the victims, and the perpetrators of the attacks. Although this is a very scientific way of approaching a novel, it is a very emotional read. Another book that has caught my attention recently is 'Born on a Blue Day' by autistic savant Daniel Tammet, and I have also been inspired by several of Friedrich Nietzsche's works. Daniel Tammet's book was particularly engaging because of his unique ability to live a fully independent life and communicate effectively to others about his condition. This correlation between autism and savantism is another area which intrigues me. As well as reading, I enjoy playing my guitar and watching films. During my liberal studies lessons for the next two terms I have chosen to study music technology and 'a celebration of cinema' to build further on these hobbies.

'I have also attended relevant talks including 'heartfelt emotions' at the Wellcome Trust. It was fascinating to see what different people's views on emotions are. It was a very exciting day and I particularly enjoyed the talks by Hugo Critchley, Martin Cowie and Dylan Evans. I have thoroughly enjoyed my studies so far and I hope to get the opportunity to pursue them further at university.'

Alicia was studying A2s in English, art and sociology at school, and applied to do a foundation art course.

'A life drawing course taken in Camberwell gave me a fresh insight into the human form which I was eager to reflect in my own work. Ever since this experience I have had a strong interest in figurative work, concentrating largely on portraiture which I enhanced by a further short course taken at Croydon.

'I am fascinated by using a wide range of contrasting media, especially when combined with traditional paints and graphite. I am particularly excited by different textures, patterns and colours that can be found within new materials and have found that even simple materials have countless new ways of making marks. I am motivated by the idea of embellishment. The transformation of a blank canvas into something completely new and exciting is definitely where my passion is rooted. I love exploring mark-making, starting with a simple mark, developing, smearing, adding colour, covering it with new lines and evolving it. I am intrigued by accidental forms that occur naturally; patterns of water spillages, shapes of old dried glue, even the splattered mouthwash in a sink looks extraordinary.

'I feel that studying art foundation will help me unroll my ideas and make new discoveries that will help me produce more rounded and conceptual work in the future. I would love to carry on studying art to degree level, find my drive and not let go.'

Summing Up

- The personal statements reproduced here and in the previous chapter are not perfect but they are very good examples of how to present yourself. Each student emphasises why he or she wants to study a particular course and shows his or her commitment and motivation.

- I hope they show you the range of topics you can cover in your own personal statement and the sort of things you could include.

- Above all, your personal statement should be a written 'snapshot' of your life so far. Make sure you show your good side!

Chapter Seven

Deferred Entry – Taking a Gap Year

Case study

'I've always loved the travelling I've done and wanted to further that and experience different cultures around the world. A gap year is a unique opportunity to travel for a few months with no responsibility. There may never be another point in my life where I have the same freedom. All the clichéd reasons of becoming more mature before university and a welcome break after years of exams are also contributing factors as to why I chose to take a year out.

'I chose to defer entry after receiving university places and only asked the universities I was choosing as my firm and insurance offers. Although most universities are supportive of a gap year, from what I've heard it can sometimes deter them from offering you a place. I can't remember the universities specifically but I remember reading some prospectuses which weren't too encouraging.

'I had no problems in gaining my deferral from the two universities I asked. Leeds replied within hours and changed it on UCAS, while Manchester took a lot longer, and involved some frustrating phone calls to get them to respond, but they never suggested it was a problem and as soon as I literally got through to them they emailed back to confirm deferral. They also mentioned that they were getting a lot of deferral requests at this time, implying it was quite common practice.'

Sophie went on to study history at the University of Manchester.

Many students like Sophie decide to take a year off from their studies. They take what has now become known as the 'gap year' and when you apply to universities you can indicate on the UCAS form that you would like to be considered for a deferred entry. Olivia did this on her first application and it made no difference to the offers she received. Some students do as Sophie did and ask the university after they have been offered a conditional place. This is a question you should ask universities when you go to UCAS conventions and exhibitions.

For many students, a gap year is a welcome break from years of studying and taking examinations. But you should plan your gap year carefully to make the most of the time and opportunities it gives you. Gap years are not an excuse to laze around and do nothing!

Gap year fairs are held throughout the country and you'll find a list of these at www.isco.org.uk. Entry is free of charge to schools and students.

Gap year sports

If you are interested in sport, you can play, coach and gain a coaching qualification in many sports projects. These projects cost anything from £1,000 to £6,000 for 4-12 weeks. Most candidates plan a year ahead of when they want to go and fundraise to cover the costs. Food and accommodation are included, but not flights.

For more information about sports during your gap year contact www.sportingopportunities.com or visit www.skillsactive.com.

If you are a good swimmer it is really useful to take the lifeguard's qualification (NPLQ), which means you could apply for jobs in all sorts of places, from holiday camps to leisure centre pools. To find out more go to www.lifeguardskills.co.uk.

Time out for travel

Travelling is an education in itself; an opportunity to see parts of the world that don't feature in holiday brochures, to explore new ways of living and to spend time with people who have a very different culture to your own. Having to earn the money to pay for your trip, plan your itinerary, sort out visas and make sure you have the correct jabs is excellent training for the future.

Some people like to join an organised project to work on for a couple of months and then travel afterwards, but these can be very expensive indeed. If this is the type of thing you would like to do, it's worth doing your homework on the companies involved.

In some places students have been accepted on a project and local people have lost their jobs (which are perhaps very difficult to come by in their area and they may be supporting extended families). There have also been incidences of projects making no actual difference to the community! Some students have found that the support they thought they were paying for was virtually non-existent. So do your homework.

For gap year volunteering opportunities, log on to www.realgap.co.uk. Their database facilities are free to all users.

Work experience in your chosen field of study

This is a very good use of your time and may help you with your university application. One young woman I know of worked in a dental surgery for a year after her A2 results, during which time she applied to and was offered a place on a prestigious course to study dentistry.

If you are planning to study archaeology, getting experience on digs will definitely help you. Try to think 'out of the box' when looking for work experience. Something that interests you and shows commitment and imagination will also stand you in good stead after you have graduated and are looking for your first proper job.

As mentioned earlier, many students who wish to study medicine get valuable experience by working on a health project overseas. You should always mention on your personal statement any plans you have for your gap year, especially if they are relevant to the degree you want to study for.

Working to fund your studies

Many students decide to take a year out to work and save money for their studies. If that is the case for you, you need to look at jobs which pay the most money. It may mean working long hours at quite boring jobs, but it will be worth it financially.

You will have to discuss with your parents whether they will expect you to make a financial contribution to the household while you are working, or perhaps you can agree to do certain chores around the house or babysit for them.

Loss of motivation to study

Case study

'As part of my gap year I took a water sports instructor course on the Isle of Wight and then worked in Sharm el Sheik. When I came back I felt very differently about going to university. I felt I was going because people said I should rather than because I really wanted to. I was definitely guided in most of my decisions by parents, teachers and friends. I didn't sit down and ask "what do I want to do?"

'Having a gap year influenced me because it showed me other options – but it also made me worry about going to university and getting into debt, and it made me anxious about what to do after graduation. I still want to study and I am keeping my university place until I have come to a decision. Nothing's definite yet. In a way, now that I am out of the school environment, I wish I'd waited and applied this year.'

Rahim has a deferred place at Leeds to study English literature and language.

For some students like Rahim, stepping out of the education system can make them see things differently and make them question whether they really do want a degree. Other students get out of the habit of studying and just don't want to go back to it. For those who have been working and earning what seems like a good wage, the prospect of being an impoverished student holds no attraction.

If this happens to you, try to think back to what motivated you in the beginning to apply to university. What made you want to do that course? Start reading about your chosen subject again and see if your previous enthusiasm returns. Contact your friends who are already at university and perhaps visit them to see if that reactivates your motivation.

If you already think you would find it difficult to go back to studying but do want to take a degree, you might be better off taking a gap year after graduation and before you find full-time work. The sort of experience you can then pick up will make a huge difference to how prospective employers view you.

Tips for parents

- In whichever way your son or daughter decides to spend their gap year, it is important to be involved so you can spur them on and prevent them from allowing time to trickle away without actually achieving anything.

- If you expect them to pay some money towards the household expenses, say so right from the beginning and negotiate a fair deal.

- Instead of payment, you could ask them to help with the chores around the house.

- Try not to be too envious when they start planning their itinerary!

Summing Up

- Deferring your entry to university and taking a gap year can be a wonderful opportunity to broaden your experiences and mature.

- Young people who plan wisely can have a great time and look forward to beginning their university course at the end of the year.

- For more information see *Gap Years – The Essential Guide* (Need2Know).

Chapter Eight

Interviews and Offers

Once your application has been made, you will be given an identification (ID) number and will be able to log on to Track at any time to see if there has been any change in your status. If you are offered an interview, you will be contacted directly by the university – this can be by email, letter or even by phone. So remember to check your emails regularly!

UCAS status email

When something changes on your application – that is when you receive an offer or are declined – you will receive an email from UCAS alerting you to this. You then log on to Track to see what has happened.

For this reason, it is crucial for you to update your UCAS records with any change of address, email or phone number.

The earlier your application goes in, the sooner you are likely to have responses.

Problems with your application

Sometimes – though not often – students find that although they have done everything they can do to make a really good application, something beyond their control goes wrong.

Late reference

One student I spoke to found that although he had completed his application early, it had not been filed because his college tutor had still not completed his reference. Before Christmas he chased this up with the person concerned and assumed they would then do it straightaway. In fact his tutor did not complete the reference section until the 15th January – the last date for applications! By this time some of the institutions the student was applying to had already allocated many of their places.

The only thing you can do in this situation is stay on the case and, if necessary, make an appointment with the college principal. It may be that your college or school has fewer students applying to university and tutors are unaware of the necessity to file applications as early as possible. You may need your parents to help you here.

Unexpected rejection

Laura applied to the University of Nottingham's school of Nursing and Midwifery. Within days of submitting her application she received a letter of rejection. The letter suggested she apply for mental health and so rewrite her personal statement to reflect this change of course!

Laura rang the person who sent the letter, who was rude and hurtful ('there were better candidates'). Laura has nine A/A* grades at GCSE and AAABB at AS. Her school was not happy with the letter either and contacted a liaison officer responsible for such matters. The liaison officer was based in London and not assigned just to the University of Nottingham. She made enquiries, but eventually Laura managed to speak to someone else at Nottingham.

This person told Laura that she had failed on account of her personal statement, which did not show commitment to midwifery. Laura asked her to read the first paragraph, which clearly showed commitment. As it was read the person 'ummed' and 'aahed' and then said she was not responsible for the rejection.

She then said they'd managed to organise an interview at Mansfield Hospital for her. Would she go? Laura agreed, although at the open day she had been told that Mansfield was for mature students who lived locally.

After a few days Laura decided that going for an interview for a course she didn't want to study was pointless – she wanted to go to the University of Nottingham. But before she did anything about this her head teacher received a call from the University of Nottingham and was told that Laura's personal statement scored 7/10 as it did not show communication skills. The Head referred her to a paragraph which gave clear evidence that this could not be true. The Head was then told that the interview at Mansfield was actually for a place at Nottingham. Laura was interviewed there and received an offer of CCC two days later!

Meanwhile the Head had set in motion an official complaint. A reply was received in January which fudged the issue – it did agree that the initial rejection letter suggesting mental health was inappropriate, however there was no explanation about the rejection itself, interview and offer.

Interviews

Fewer institutions now offer interviews to candidates, but some invite applicants to a course open day. For some universities, for instance Oxford and Cambridge, and for some courses like medicine, interviews will be obligatory. You will also find that some universities like to interview or audition candidates for music and drama courses.

If you are offered an interview, the university will contact you directly by email, letter or phone. You may or may not be given a choice of dates. If you cannot attend on a particular date you should contact the admissions tutor immediately to rearrange if possible.

Before the interview

It is essential that you prepare yourself well for your interview – this is your chance to convince the university department that you are right for the course. So you need to:

- Read around the subject, including relevant newspaper articles.

- Think about your opinions on key issues and consider how you will express them.

'My advice to parents and Year 13 pupils who are unhappy about a rejection is to pursue the university for an explanation, first via the liaison officer and then further. It is best to have the support of the head teacher as well. In my opinion too many universities reject or accept without being held to account.'

Laura's mother whose two older children have both been to university.

- Make notes of questions you could be asked (see page 79).

- Find out as much as possible about the course at this institution – make sure you have read all the relevant information in the prospectus and checked course profiles.

- Think about and write down questions to ask them (see page 79).

On the day of the interview

Plan your route so that you arrive in plenty of time. If the interviews begin early in the day, you may need to arrange accommodation for the night before. In any case, allow yourself 'emergency time' so that if anything goes wrong en route you should still get there in time. It doesn't matter if you arrive too early, you can always explore the student union facilities.

Make an effort with your appearance. You don't have to wear clothes you wouldn't be seen dead in, but neither should you turn up as though you've spent the night clubbing! Wear something you feel comfortable in and something that makes you feel good and you know suits you. If you are applying to study drama, you could be asked to wear or bring clothes that you feel comfortable moving around in, as you may be requested to take part in improvisations or workshops.

At the interview

Try to appear relaxed even if you don't feel it. The lecturers interviewing you know you will probably be feeling nervous and will make allowances for this. Try to breathe deeply and slowly to calm yourself and if a question completely throws you, ask them to repeat it to give you time to think. Or just say you don't understand and it will be up to them to ask it in another way.

To help with your breathing, sit up straight and don't slouch. Maintain a degree of eye contact and try to smile now and again!

Answer their questions in full sentences and don't be tempted to exaggerate or lie about your achievements – you may be asked for proof. One candidate said he'd designed and set up a website for a community group. The interviewer immediately passed over a laptop and asked him to log on to the site, which he did as, fortunately, he had been telling the truth!

Questions you could be asked:

* What made you choose this course/university?

* What is your understanding of this concept?

* What do you intend to gain from doing this course?

* What qualities can you bring to this course?

* What is your opinion of this recent development?

* What do you see yourself doing in 10 years time?

* In your personal statement you say that you . . . tell me about this?

* Tell me about your part-time job in . . . ?

* Can you tell me about your school?

* Do you think single sex education/co-education a good idea?

Questions you could ask:

Always prepare questions to ask, including:

* Details of course structure.

* How your work would be assessed.

* How much contact time students have.

* What sort of careers graduates from this course go into.

* Types of student accommodation.

If you come away kicking yourself for forgetting to ask a question that is really important to you, you can always email when you get home!

Non-academic reasons for rejection after an interview

A quick glance through chapter 7 'Subject Tables' in Brian Heap's book *Degree Course Offers* reveals the frequency of the major reasons why some candidates are not offered a place. These include:

- Candidates late for interview.
- Lack of interest, enthusiasm, motivation or commitment.
- Poor language skills.
- Lack of knowledge about the course.
- Lack of clarity about personal goals.

Invitations to course days

Many universities do not offer interviews, but once they have made you an offer they will invite you to a course open day. This is a chance for you to hear about what is being offered and the type of work you'll be expected to do. You'll get a tour of the department and get a chance to meet the staff and students.

The university, having offered you a place, is now selling itself to you. They are hoping you will make them your firm choice so will be on their best behaviour! It is also an opportunity for you to look at the place (if you haven't visited on an open day) and see if you can imagine yourself living and studying there.

You will be able to ask questions and meet other students who have also been offered a place. Keep some notes of your thoughts while you are there so you can compare and contrast courses you have been offered.

Replying to your offers

You do not have to do anything or respond in any way (unless you want to) until you have received a reply from all five universities you have applied to. The replies will be: conditional (on you achieving certain grades) or unsuccessful.

You then have to make your decision. You must accept two universities: one is a firm acceptance and the other is your insurance place – one that is asking for lower grades. You make your replies online in Track. Each of your choices has a reply box alongside it. Click on to this and there are three options: firm, insurance and decline.

If you have applied after having received your exam results, your offers will be unconditional – meaning you have achieved the criteria they demand – and then you accept one as your firm choice – the one you will be going to!

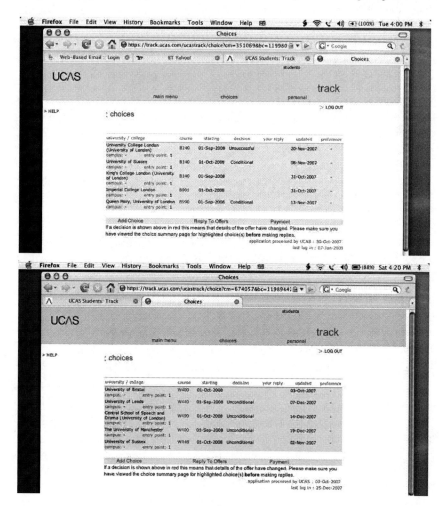

Changing your mind – withdrawing your application

Case study

'I had first decided to study English and drama combined studies, as I was told that although drama was my passion – English would make my degree more academic. English was always a subject I enjoyed but it never excited me as much as drama, and deep down I think I knew it would be a mistake to take this degree. I attended a course open day at a university that had offered me a place, and this confirmed all my beliefs – this really wasn't the degree for me.

'I then withdrew my application from UCAS independently, which gave me a whole year to choose another degree – but it only confirmed that I really did want to study drama. For me it was not a hard decision to withdraw my application as I was already intending to take a gap year and I had applied for deferred entry anyway.

'Repeatedly I was told that drama wasn't a "proper" degree and often when I told people what I was hoping to study they would say "oh, another actress". I was put out by other's disbelief in my degree choice, however with the help of my mother and my drama teacher, I was able to overcome this and retaliate, defending my choice of degree.

'Since then, I have reapplied a year later to study drama and have accepted a place at the University of Manchester. I found it much simpler applying with my grades as I knew exactly where to apply to, and am now very much looking forward to my gap year travels this year and attending Manchester in September.'

Olivia went on to study drama at the University of Manchester.

You can withdraw your application at any time but you cannot reapply for the same course again at one of the universities you chose the first time around. Withdrawing when you have already planned a gap year makes life easier. If you haven't planned a deferred entry, you will have to think about what you are going to do during this year (see chapter 7).

Extra

This is a route you can take if you have made your five choices, have received decisions from all of them and have either had no offers or have turned down the ones you have received.

In Extra you can apply for one other course at a time using the Track service on the UCAS website. You can use this facility from the end of February until the end of June while you are in Year 13.

How to use Extra

Log on to your Track screen and if you become eligible for Extra, you should see a new button. This will enable you to see which courses still have places available through Course Search. It's a good idea to then check with the university or college that they will consider you.

Just as you would have checked the entry profile for your first five choices, do so again for this course. If in your original application you chose very popular courses, it would be wise to look for one that is less in demand or to think about another type of course. For instance, politics courses are very popular and you need high grades, but if you combine politics with, say, East Asian studies, the qualifications required will be lower.

Once you have made a decision, enter the details on your Track screen and your application will be sent to that institution.

Receiving an offer via Extra

If the university makes you an offer, you have to decide whether you want to accept it. If you do, you cannot apply anywhere else and you need to reply by the date shown on Track. However, if you decide not to accept the offer (perhaps you think it is too high for you to achieve), or your application to that institution is unsuccessful, your Extra button on Track will be reactivated and you can try again if you have time. If this fails, you will be able to apply through the Clearing process after you have received your examination results.

Late applications

It is possible – though not particularly advisable – to make an application through UCAS up until the end of June. After this, applications are made via Clearing only. If you make a late application, you will not have the full choice of places on offer but you may, like Lily, find exactly what you are looking for.

Tips for parents

- This is an extremely stressful time for university applicants (and their parents!) and you may need to mop up a few tears if your offspring doesn't get an offer from the university they have set their heart on.

- Keep positive – offer advice if asked for or just a hug of commiseration.

- If there are problems you think you should help with, contact the sixth form tutor in the first instance.

'I didn't want to go to university but then I heard a talk given by a lecturer from Westminster University and realised that this was exactly the course I would like to do. My college was really helpful and I applied at the last minute – only to Westminster – and was offered a place. I'm really happy there.'

Lily, second year undergraduate in music management.

Summing Up

- If there is a problem (like a late reference or early rejection) you should consult your parents and school advisers. They will be able to help.

- Prepare well for any interviews you are offered and take the opportunity to visit the department if you are invited to a course open day.

- Don't panic if you change your mind about the course you have applied for. It's much better to find this out before you actually start your degree! You may have to delay for a year but you can put that time to good use. Or you could try going through Clearing.

- Remember that if you do not get any offers or you decline the ones that you do receive, you can make a further application through Extra.

- If you decide university is for you after the initial deadline, late applications are possible and you may still find an appropriate course.

Chapter Nine

Getting Your Results

The A level results come out in mid-August while other results like BTec and IB come out earlier. You need to be available if you don't get the results you'd hoped for!

At most schools and sixth form colleges, students go in to collect their results and are given a time from which these will be available. The universities receive these results the day before you do. If you want a sneak preview of how well you've done, log on to your tracking page on the UCAS site. One of my daughter's friends did this and discovered that her offer from the University of Exeter had gone from 'conditional' to 'accepted'. She didn't know her exact grades but knew that she must have achieved the three Bs of her offer.

Getting your offer grades

Congratulations! In the next few days your offer will be confirmed.

What if you don't get the grades you need?

After you have received all the replies from the universities you have applied to, you will have accepted your first choice and an insurance choice which offers lower grades. (If you have received no offers, you would have gone through Extra, see page 83.)

However, you may have set your heart on your first choice – and haven't quite achieved the grades. So what do you do?

- First of all, don't panic. If your school has tutors ready to help you, make use of them! Discuss your results and ask for their advice.

- It might be worth phoning the admissions tutors to see if they will still accept you with lower grades. Your results slip will give you a breakdown of your marks so you will be able to see if you have just missed out on a grade that is crucial to your offer. You have nothing to lose from this and possibly a place to gain!

- If your grades are lower than both offers, and you have been unable to persuade either institution to accept you, you can go through the Clearing system. The sooner you start this, the better. All places which are yet to be filled are available to see online and you should work through these with a tutor or a parent.

- If your grades are significantly lower than those predicted, you, your parents and your teachers may decide that one or some of your papers should be re-marked. There is a limited timeframe for this and it does not always work in your favour. However, I know one student who had a D re-graded to an A and her first choice then accepted her!

- You may, however, decide that you would rather retake parts of the examinations to try to improve your grades. This will involve sorting out tutoring and reapplying to university for the following year.

Case study

'I took biology, economics and history at A2 and needed three Bs to study biology at Warwick. My results were BCC and I didn't feel very good about it. I decided not to accept my insurance offer as I hadn't visited the university. I had already planned to take a year off, so I decided to resit two biology and two history papers and reapply. I have applied to Warwick again and four others. And this time I'm going to visit the universities I get offers from. I think I should have done that the first time round.' Jake.

What if you get better grades than your offer grades?

Sometimes students accept a certain course because they don't think they will be able to get higher grades, but each year some applicants pass their exams with better results than expected. And this may mean that some will have not only met the conditions of their firm choice, but will have exceeded them. UCAS have introduced Adjustment for these applicants – it provides an opportunity for them to reconsider where and what to study.

If you want to use Adjustment, you will need to register in Track. The option to register will be displayed for all applicants whose place has been confirmed.

The Adjustment process is available from A level results day until 31st August. From this time you have a maximum of five calendar days (five 24 hour periods, including Saturdays and Sundays) to register and secure an alternative course, if you decide this is what you want to do.

If you want to try to find an alternative course you must register to use Adjustment so universities and colleges can view your application.

Your Track 'choices' page shows you when your Adjustment period ends. If you become eligible to use Adjustment less than five calendar days before 31st August, you have the remaining time before then to find an alternative place.

If you do not find a suitable place elsewhere you will remain accepted at your original choice.

Clearing

Figures from UCAS show that in 2006, 500,000 web searches were counted on the first day of Clearing – 44,000 of which were in the first half an hour! The most popular courses searched for in Clearing were psychology, economics, English and medicine.

More than 26,600 students gained a university place through Clearing in 2012, but, as you can see, the sooner you apply, the more chance you have of gaining a place you would like.

In newspapers you will also see courses which still have places available. UCAS has awarded *The Telegraph* the rights to publish UCAS Clearing Listings.

Changed course offers

Some universities may offer you an alternative course to the one you originally applied for but missed the grades on – for example you may have applied for psychology and be offered psychology and sociology as a combined course. This might be worth considering as it may have been the university itself that you liked most and you can retain your accommodation first year guarantee. These are called 'changed course offers' and universities are allowed to do this if you have not met the conditions of their offer. Take time to consider any alternative offers and visit or speak to university staff and careers advisers in school/college if possible.

Tips for parents

- Parents should make every effort to ensure they are not away on holiday or business at this time and, if possible, you should have a day's holiday from work so you can be there for any eventuality.

- Although your son or daughter probably won't want you to go with them to collect the results – and are likely to be celebrating with their friends in the evening – they may need you there to share their success or support them if the results aren't what they anticipated.

- Have some sort of celebration prepared in advance – and do it whatever the results.

- If the results aren't good, don't start criticising their lack of preparation or revision – this is not the time for recriminations, just parental support.

Summing Up

■ Getting your results can be almost as stressful as sitting the exams! Remember all your achievements so far and try to think of these exams as another step along the way.

■ Try to stay calm and open your envelope away from your friends so you can take in the results properly. If you want to shout for joy or shed a tear, do so.

■ If your results are a disappointment, go and see your sixth form tutor or any teacher available, who can help you sort out what to do. Remember that places in Clearing may go in record time. There are other options apart from Clearing and it may take you a while to decide what you want to do. Don't worry about what other people think, do what's best for you.

Chapter Ten

Thinking About Money

One of the things you will have to consider is how you will support yourself during your studies. Many young people worry about the amount of debt they will have acquired by the time they finish their course. Some careful planning is needed to manage your finances and you may be eligible for loans, grants and bursaries.

You should receive information on grants and loans through the post and some schools will offer advice and help. You can begin applying in the March of the year you begin university.

For more in-depth information about student finance, see *Student Finance: The Essential Guide* (Need2Know).

Student loans

You can apply for a student loan to cover the full cost of your tuition fees up to the maximum of £9,000. This is not means-tested, in other words the amount you get is not related to your parents' income. This is paid directly to your university or college.

You can also apply for a loan to go towards your living costs. This does depend on your personal circumstances and how much your household has in income. This money will be paid directly to you in three instalments.

You do not have to start repaying these loans until you are in employment and earning over £21,000 per year.

'No one should be put off higher education because of worries about student debt.'

Martin Lewis, 'Talking Money – a parent's guide to student finance', www.moneysavingexpert. com.

Maintenance grants

From September 2012 more students will be able to apply for a grant towards their living expenses, as the government has raised the amount of income a household can earn and still qualify for a student grant. You do not have to pay this money back.

Students from a household with an income of up to £25,000 will get a full grant (£3,250 a year in 2012) and partial maintenance grants are available to students from families with incomes between £25,000 and £42,600.

* These figures are correct at the time of going to press but should be confirmed with Student Finance nearer the time (see below for contact details).

Bursaries and scholarships

There are also bursaries you may be entitled to and do not have to repay. For instance, some universities reward academic achievement. Also, if you are in receipt of the maximum maintenance grant, universities charging the highest rate of fees will also give you a non-repayable bursary. To find out more you should check with the university or college you have an offer from.

For more information you need to contact:

- Student Finance England on 0845 300 5090. You can call Monday to Friday, 8am-8pm and Saturday and Sunday from 9am-5.30pm. You can also visit the website at www.direct.gov.uk/en/Dl1/Directories/UsefulContactsByCategory/EducationAndLearningContacts/DG_172310.

- Student Finance NI on 0845 600 0662. You can call Monday to Friday from 8am-8pm and Saturday and Sunday from 9am-5.30pm. You can also visit the website at www.studentfinanceni.co.uk.

- Student Awards Agency for Scotland (SAAS) on 0300 555 0505. You can call every day from 8.30am-5pm (4.30pm on Fridays). From June to mid-October you will be able to call every day until 6pm (4.30pm on Fridays). You can also visit the website at www.saas.gov.uk.

- Student Finance Wales on 0845 602 8845. You can call Monday to Friday from 8am-8pm and Saturday from 9am-1pm. The helpline is closed on Sundays. You can also visit the website at www.studentfinancewales.co.uk.

To see if you are eligible for a scholarship go to www.scholarship-search.org.uk.

Financial implications of where you go to study

In a recent survey, the Royal Bank of Scotland cites Leeds as top of the most cost-effective university cities (which can save a student up to £75 per week), and Nottingham as the least cost-effective. Leeds came out on top because students there also have access to part-time work.

How expensive a city is to live in may influence your choice.

The Student Living Index compiled by the Royal Bank of Scotland lists the top five cities for students to live in (from a financial point of view) as Leeds, Brighton, Dundee, London and Liverpool.

Financial advice

If you come from a low-income or one-parent family, you could visit www.egas-online.org. This is an organisation which promotes access to education for students who otherwise would not be able to continue in full-time education.

They have a downloadable questionnaire for you to fill in. Once they've received this, they will provide an individual written response which will outline the statutory funding and benefits you are entitled to.

There is also excellent financial advice on Martin Lewis' Money Saving Expert website:

www.moneysavingexpert.com/health/student-finance

www.moneysavingexpert.com/banking/Student-bank-account

The advice on student bank accounts is updated annually every July/August as soon as all the new details are announced.

Paying back your loan

You will begin to pay back your loan once you are earning above £21,000; you will pay 9 pence for every extra pound you earn. If you earn less than £21,000 or are unemployed you will not make repayments. After 30 years, any amount outstanding will be written off.

Tips for parents

- If your household income is less than £25,000, your son or daughter will be able to apply for a non-repayable grant.

- Martin Lewis has written an informative leaflet about student finance for parents; go to his website mentioned on page 95 for more details.

Summing Up

- There are many ways for you to finance your studies, which may include part-time work during term time, student loans and grants. For more information on student finance, see *Student Finance: The Essential Guide* (Need2Know).

- Whatever you do, don't be put off going to university because you are afraid of running up huge debts. Make sure you plan and budget properly so you minimise what you may eventually owe.

- Finally, for more information about university life, see *University: A Survival Guide* (Need2Know).

Appendix One

The UCAS Timetable

Below are the most important dates to consider for your university application. The ones marked with * never change. The other dates are subject to confirmation and you should check the UCAS website nearer the time. Visit www.ucas.com.

- **September***   You can start your application process.
- **15 October***   Deadline for applications to Oxford University, University of Cambridge and courses in medicine, dentistry and veterinary science or veterinary medicine.
- **15 January***   Applications must be in to guarantee equal academic consideration. This is the last date for most on time applications.
- **16 January to 30 June***   Late applications received by UCAS are forwarded to institutions for consideration at their discretion.
- **25 February**   You can refer yourself through Extra for the first time.
- **31 March**   Universities and colleges should aim to have sent their decisions on all applications received by 15 January.
- **30 June***   Last date for receipt of applications for immediate consideration. Those received after this date are held for Clearing.
- **3 July**   Last date for applicants to refer themselves through Extra.
- **August**   Publication of SQA results.
- **August**   Publication of GCE and VCE results. Start of vacancy information service.
- **20 September***   Last date to submit an application.

Dates correct at the time of going to press. To confirm, or to find out more, log on to www.ucas.com/students/importantdates

Appendix Two

Glossary of UCAS Terms

Below is a list of commonly used words and phrases that appear in the UCAS application, together with a summary of what they mean.

Adjustment: applicants who have met and exceeded the conditions of their firm choice are given an opportunity to look for an alternative place while holding their original confirmed place.

Apply: the online application system for applying for higher education courses. Apply and its supporting information can be accessed on the UCAS website.

Clearing: a system used towards the end of the academic cycle. If you have not secured a place, it enables you to apply for course vacancies.

Conditional offer: an offer made by a university or college, whereby you must fulfil certain criteria before you can be accepted on the relevant course.

Confirmation: when conditional offers that you have accepted become unconditional or are declined. Confirmation is dependent on your qualification/exam results.

Deferral: holding an offer until the following year.

Entry Profiles: comprehensive information about individual courses and institutions, including statistics and entry requirements. Entry profiles are found on Course Search on the UCAS website.

Extra: the opportunity to apply for another course if you have used all five choices and not secured a place.

Firm offer: the offer that you have accepted as your first choice.

Institution: a university or college offering higher education courses.

Insurance offer: the offer that you have accepted as your second choice, in case you do not meet the requirements for your firm offer.

Personal ID number: a 10-digit individual number assigned to you when you register to use Apply. The number is displayed in the format 123-456-7890.

Point of entry: your year of entry to the course, for example, 2 refers to the second year of the course.

Track: a system where you can track the progress of your application online, reply to any offers received, and make certain amendments, for example change of address or email.

Unconditional offer: an offer given to you by a university or college if you have satisfied the criteria and can attend the course.

Unsuccessful: you have not been accepted by the university or college concerned.

Withdrawal: either you or a university / college cancels a choice before a decision has been made – a reason will be included if the withdrawal was issued by an institution.

Help List

For help with your university application

UCAS

Tel: 0871 468 0 468, open Monday to Friday, 8.30am-6pm
enquiries@ucas.ac.uk
www.ucas.com
UCAS is the UK central organisation through which applications are processed
for entry to higher education. You can research courses using Course Search,
make your application using Apply and follow the progress of your application
using Track.

Calendar of university open days

www.opendays.com

This website can help you find out when the open days are for the universities
you'd like to visit. Search for a university or browse the open day calendar. You
can email queries via the website.

Careers information

Connexions Direct

www.connexionsdirect.co.uk
Connexions Direct have a careers database, which groups careers into
families. This gives you a broad insight into the type of jobs available in any
particular area, and the qualifications and personal qualities required.

Comparison sites

BachelorsPortal.eu

www.bachelorsportal.eu
This site gives a comprehensive list of universities and courses in Europe, the fees they charge, length of study and the qualifications necessary.

Guardian Education

www.educationguardian.co.uk
At Guardian Education, universities are rated by a range of criteria, including staff/student ratio, money spent per student, teaching, feedback and job prospects. You can email your queries via the website.

The Push Guide

www.push.co.uk/pushguide
The Push Guide is a student site which 'tells it like it is'. It's an independent guide to UK universities, covering university league tables, top tens and includes a 'uni chooser'.

The Sunday Times University Guide

www.timesonline.co.uk
From the main webpage, click on 'Lifestyle', 'Education' and then 'Sunday Times University Guide'. This guide compares universities by student satisfaction, research quality, staff/student ratio, money spent on services and facilities, entry standards, students completing the course, good honours and graduate prospects. Email queries via website.

Unistats

www.unistats.com
The Unistats website is designed to allow you to compare universities and colleges in the UK. Authoritative, official information is brought together to help you make an informed choice.

Financial information

Hotcourses – Student Money

www.scholarship-search.org.uk
To see if you are eligible for a scholarship or for advice on budget planning and loan repayment, visit this website. You can search by subject or organisation, and can email queries via the website.

Money Saving Expert

www.moneysavingexpert.com/banking/student-bank-account
www.moneysavingexpert.com/health/student-finance
Martin Lewis' Money Saving Expert site gives excellent advice on student bank accounts, but is also worth visiting for other money-saving information.

Student Finance

Student Finance England
Tel: 0845 300 5090
www.direct.gov.uk/studentfinance
The helpline is available Monday to Friday from 8am-8pm and Saturday and Sunday from 9am-5.30pm.

Student Finance NI
Tel: 0845 600 0662
www.studentfinanceni.co.uk
The helpline is available Monday to Friday from 8am-8pm and Saturday and Sunday from 9am-5.30pm.

Student Awards Agency for Scotland (SAAS)
Tel: 0300 555 0505
www.saas.gov.uk
The helpline is available every day from 8am-5pm (4.30pm on Fridays). However, from early June to mid-October it is available every day from 8am-6pm (4.30pm on Fridays).

Student Finance Wales
Tel: 0845 602 8845
www.studentfinancewales.co.uk

The helpline is available Monday to Friday from 8am-8pm and Saturday from 9am-1pm. It is closed on Sundays.

These are official websites for applying for student finance. They administer the payment of financial support for students, incorporating the whole process, from promotion and assessment to payment and collection.

Gap year information

Gap Sports

Sporting Opportunities, The Clock House, Station Approach, Marlow, Buckinghamshire, SL7 1NT
Tel: 0208 123 8702
info@gapsports.com
www.gapsports.com

For information about sports during your gap year contact Gap Sports. They provide coaching placements, sports courses, training programmes and sports adventure tours abroad. They also have volunteer projects for the less sporty.

Independent Schools Careers Service (ISCO)

St George's House, Knoll Road, Camberley, Surrey, GU15 3SY
Tel: 01276 687500
www.isco.org.uk

ISCO is the independent schools careers service from The Inspiring Futures Foundation. It provides careers education and guidance for young people. The site also offers details of gap year fairs open to the public.

Real Gap

TUI Travel House, Crawley Business Quarter, Fleming Way, Crawley, West Sussex RH10 9QL
Tel: 01892 882 676
www.realgap.co.uk

Skills Active

Head Office: 020 7632 2000

Northern Ireland: 028 9756 2007
Scotland: 0131 339 7869
Wales: 029 2044 4150
skills@skillsactive.com
www.skillsactive.com
Skills Active helps people to improve their level of skills and is committed to the needs of volunteers.

For students with disabilities

Skill: National Bureau for Students with Disabilities

www.skill.org.uk
This is a national charity promoting opportunities for young people and adults with any kind of impairment in post-16 education, training and employment. There is also an information booklet 'Applying to Higher Education: Guidance for Disabled People' that you can download for free. Also lots of links to other useful websites.

Need - 2 - Know

Available Titles Include ...

Allergies A Parent's Guide
ISBN 978-1-86144-064-8 £8.99

Autism A Parent's Guide
ISBN 978-1-86144-069-3 £8.99

Blood Pressure The Essential Guide
ISBN 978-1-86144-067-9 £8.99

Dyslexia and Other Learning Difficulties
A Parent's Guide ISBN 978-1-86144-042-6 £8.99

Bullying A Parent's Guide
ISBN 978-1-86144-044-0 £8.99

Epilepsy The Essential Guide
ISBN 978-1-86144-063-1 £8.99

Your First Pregnancy The Essential Guide
ISBN 978-1-86144-066-2 £8.99

Gap Years The Essential Guide
ISBN 978-1-86144-079-2 £8.99

Secondary School A Parent's Guide
ISBN 978-1-86144-093-8 £9.99

Primary School A Parent's Guide
ISBN 978-1-86144-088-4 £9.99

Applying to University The Essential Guide
ISBN 978-1-86144-052-5 £8.99

ADHD The Essential Guide
ISBN 978-1-86144-060-0 £8.99

Student Cookbook – Healthy Eating The Essential Guide
ISBN 978-1-86144-069-3 £8.99

Multiple Sclerosis The Essential Guide
ISBN 978-1-86144-086-0 £8.99

Coeliac Disease The Essential Guide
ISBN 978-1-86144-087-7 £9.99

Special Educational Needs A Parent's Guide
ISBN 978-1-86144-116-4 £9.99

The Pill An Essential Guide
ISBN 978-1-86144-058-7 £8.99

University A Survival Guide
ISBN 978-1-86144-072-3 £8.99

View the full range at **www.need2knowbooks.co.uk**.
To order our titles call **01733 898103**, email **sales@
n2kbooks.com** or visit the website. Selected ebooks
available online.

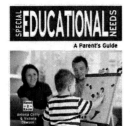
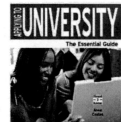
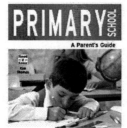

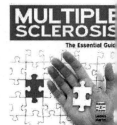

Need - 2 - Know, Remus House, Coltsfoot Drive, Peterborough, PE2 9BF